WHEN LEADERS LIVE
TOGETHER

How Two Strong Personalities Can
Thrive In Marriage

WHEN LEADERS LIVE
TOGETHER

How Two Strong Personalities Can
Thrive In Marriage

LARRY
TITUS

DEVI
TITUS

HIGHERLIFE
DEVELOPMENT SERVICES, INC.

Oviedo, Florida

When Leaders Live Together
By Larry Titus—Devi Titus

Published by HigherLife Development Services, Inc.
400 Fontana Circle
Building 1, Suite 105
Oviedo, FL 32765
(407) 563-4806
www.ahigherlife.com

ISBN 13: 978-1-93524-573-5
ISBN 10: 1935245732

Cover Design: Dave Whitlock

First Edition

12 13 14 15 16 — 9 8 7 6 5 4 3 2 1
Printed in the United States of America

TABLE of CONTENTS

FOREWORD
By: Larry

EVI AND I have been married 48 years. As happens quite often, we will again be away on our anniversary, this time in Brazil. When we got married, I told her that I would show her the world, and by God's grace, I've done a pretty good job. Of course, I didn't tell how opulent it would be, or how lavish the travel plans were, whether we'd be riding in a limousine or a putt-putt; I just told her that I would show her the world.

The "world" has included sleeping on dirty sheets in India, boards for beds in Thailand, riding on an out-of-control bus as it careens down an icy road in Colorado, squeezed into the back seat of taxis with three other people in Nigeria, sharing rooms with creepy-crawly-critters in more than one place, and yes, having more than our share of beautiful hotels where we felt spoiled by God.

The bottom line is that Devi has always been by my side, whether with princes or peons. She has never complained, never has she tried to run an independent course, seeking her own professional agenda, nor tried to usurp my authority. And, one as talented as Devi would have no problem succeeding in just about anything she set her mind to.

So, our marriage has always been the two of us acting as one. We have chosen to act in tandem, with each one of us leading at times, rather than living together separately and independently.

This book is all about marriage, but marriage of a different kind. We have not tried to write the stock marriage book, addressing the usual problems. There are a plethora of good books on marriage, books that will answer about any problem that might arise in your marriage. But there seems to be a paucity of books written about headship and what it means, about how strong personalities can work together in unity, how each of the partners can lead in their area of expertise, and how couples can reverse the demonic trend of divorce and shallow relationships that's epidemic in our society, and present a healthy example of Jesus and His Church to a seeking and sick world.

As you will notice, there are more personal anecdotes than you might be accustomed to in such a book, but we've done that so you can see the practicality of what we're prescribing. This book is both theological and practical. It's possible to put the biblical injunctions for couples into a template that allows them to live out their God-given marriage mandate in the modern world and succeed. After all, if our marriage doesn't function in harmony, how will people accurately see Jesus and His Church? For marriage is to be modeled after Jesus and His Church.

Lastly, this book carries a tinge of the unique in that Devi's leadership skills are in many ways much superior to mine. *When Leaders Live Together* has not been written by a strong Choleric, dominate Alpha male type; I'm just one of those ordinary personalities that make up nearly 70 percent of men. Yet I, like all men, have leadership skills in some area. The same is true of women. Regardless of her personality type, she still has leadership gifts in a specific area, whether great or small. So, this book inherently carries comfort for both spouses; no matter what percentage your leadership skills are, docile or dominant, passive or persuasive, you are still an effective leader in some area, and worthy of encouragement.

Because I constantly teach men, I'm always concerned that the tear-down, condescending world they've been born into will continue to devalue and emasculate them. I want you to know that you're not a whit inferior, and most likely, far more superior than you give yourself credit for. For the men out there who feel that you'll never be a good head, let alone a good leader, I'm writing to let you know that you already are. Your skills just need to be recognized, encouraged and released. God designed you for greatness, so, as I tell thousands of men, "You're Awesome and you can't even help it." We want to elevate both men and women in the understanding of how special they are and how they can release their leadership skills in the most elementary, yet profound, ways.

So, welcome to a book of a different kind.

—LARRY TITUS

FOREWORD
By: Devi

WRITING THIS BOOK has been a fun journey. Many years ago, Larry and I quickly wrote the first version and self-published it so I could distribute it at a conference where I was speaking. My assigned workshop topic to ministers' wives was "Living with a Leader."

During the preparation process for that conference, I realized that I not only lived with a leader, as my husband was the senior pastor of a large congregation, but Larry lived with a leader, too. It was my intention to encourage pastors' wives in the challenges that they encounter because of their husbands' job—leading a church. Yes, while leading a church is a calling for some, it is a job for others. But when men who are leaders, regardless of what they lead, also live with a leader, it can be double trouble.

During my conversations with Larry about this topic, we decided to write a book together, each giving our personal perspective on the subject at hand. In the end, we have a marriage book of a different kind. It is not intended to be comprehensive marriage counseling. It is intended to be real, simple, and easy to understand. We have not edited out our individual style of communicating. You will see his humor and my bottom-line approach.

In some chapters, Larry writes to both the spouse and to men. First, I attempted to change his gender voice to include men and women. When I did, the script lost his passion and personality. Larry writes, "He Says" for both men and women to read, but you have to understand that's because Larry is so passionate to train men, and he often switches his directive to men only. I love this about him. He is a husband and father and talks like one most of the time. He is a pastor and talks like a pastor. He is a friend and talks to men as a friend. So, enjoy who he is as he shares his wisdom with you.

It happens that my chapters have bottom-line principles for men and women, but oftentimes, I find myself speaking to women specifically. It is natural for me to do this since I speak to thousands of women annually. So, practically speaking, our chapters reflect who we are.

Two thousand copies of our first pathetic, defective book, complete with typing errors and poor sentence structures, sold quickly. Embarrassed by its presentation, I refused to invest in a second press run of our original manuscript. Therefore, our original work has been out of print for several years. So now, we respond to demand and rewrite *When Leaders Live Together, How Two Strong Personalities Can Thrive in Marriage*. This is the expanded version by authors who now have 48 years of marriage at this publication date and lots of practice in honoring and submitting to one another as we experience "when leaders live together."

I am as passionately in love with Larry today as I was when we married and we definitely have more fun. We have learned to laugh when we notice that we are "leading" each other or should I say, telling each other what to do. There is really nothing important enough to argue about—He lets me be right and I let him be right. We do not try to prove each other wrong. Honoring Larry has been my privilege. He chose me to be his wife and I have concentrated on making life wonderful for him so he would never regret choosing me. While honoring and serving Larry, submitting to his headship, I didn't lose myself. I found myself.

Larry has loved me and faithfully served me when I didn't deserve it. His passion has taken me to many nations in the world. Tears still come to my eyes when I think about our amazing lives together—this little girl from a very small California town saying "I do—I will" and keeping my promise. My treasure is our amazing two children, grandchildren, and great grandchildren modeling the love of Christ that Larry has demonstrated in our family. I have responded to him as a faithful bride and I'm deeply grateful for the power of his love in my life. We have clung together and made it through the tough times.

Drop your guard and lay down your swords. Enjoy the incredible dynamic life that is created by leaders who love to serve one another and embrace each other's leadership. Grasp these principles and own them; make them your own. One day, you can write your own version of *When Leaders Live Together*. We anticipate hearing your stories.

GRATEFUL BRIDE,

DEVI TITUS

D o you want to know why I chose to co-author a book about "When Leaders Live Together"? It's because I needed one myself and couldn't find it. Do you know why I'm qualified to write such a book? It's because I live with a leader. No, on second thought, I live with a Leader with a capitol "L". No, I live with a LEADER! On a scale from one to ten, my wife's leadership quotient is one hundred ninety-three, and climbing daily. I want you to know, "I LIVE WITH A LEADER!!!!!" Any questions?

I remember flying on a 747 jetliner one day when she attempted to rearrange everyone's seat locations in our section of the jumbo jet. My wife wanted our family to sit together.

I remember her designing all the intricate details of our wedding. She also wants to redesign everyone else's weddings when she attends.

I remember her witnessing a traffic accident and immediately taking over at the scene. Without hesitation, she began to help the injured, direct traffic, call 911, and tell the policeman to turn on his blinking light; then, she ran down the street in hot pursuit of the hit-and-run driver. My wife accomplished all of this in a designer suit and high heels! Nothing, and I mean nothing, is impossible for my leader/wife.

Again I ask, are there any questions about my qualifications for writing a book about living with a leader? Friends, I live with Devi Titus – a gifted writer, magazine publisher, model, mother, conference speaker, teacher and preacher of the Word, interior designer, founder of the Mentoring Mansion, entrepreneur, and doer of anything she fixes her mind to accomplish.

I think Devi invented the word "Leader." She came out of her mother's womb as a leader and hasn't stopped leading for one day of her life. Then she married me. When she married me, she married a leader. However, I'm a leader out of obligation. I'm a leader because I'm the head of my wife and because I've been a pastor for thirty-four years. I'm a leader because I'm a man, and men are supposed to be leaders. I'm a leader because I have biblical convictions that cause me to lead. Finally, and most importantly, I'm a leader because my wife tells me I am. So there! Amen!

Needless to say, we've had a few disagreements over how to lead in our forty-eight years of marriage. So, that's the reason for this book. Do you or anyone you know relate to my situation? If so, join me as we discuss the rich and rewarding possibilities inherent in living with a leader.

1

[HE Says]
∞

HEADSHIP and LEADERSHIP
By: Larry

D o you know the difference between headship and leadership in marriage? The biblical responsibility of a married man to oversee his home and love, protect, and release his wife defines headship. Leadership references one's personality and/or gifting. God has called you the 'head' of your wife, if you are a married man. The dominant leader in the home, on the other hand, can be either the man or the woman. Not understanding this distinction has caused centuries of confusion in marriages. Men too often try to take on the leader role because they feel obligated to do so. Conversely, women try to subdue their leadership personalities because they feel that to lead would contradict their responsibilities to submit to their husbands.

But, I've got good news. If a man doesn't possess leadership skills, he does not have to lead out of obligation. However, he still must assume responsibility for headship. If a woman possesses natural leadership ability, she can lead freely according to her personality. However, she must not violate the headship principle through rebellion, domination, or disrespect.

MAN'S CALL TO HEADSHIP

Let's look at the following scriptures concerning the man's call to headship:

> But I want you to understand that the head of every man is Christ, the head of a wife is her husband, and the head of Christ is God. I Corinthians 11:3

> For the husband is the head of the wife even as Christ is the head of the church, his body, and is himself its Savior. Ephesians 5:23

1

In understanding headship, one must realize that man ultimately stands responsible before God for the marriage. As I mentioned above, it's a gender thing. It doesn't relate to a man's qualifications, abilities, or personality. It relates to only one thing. God, in His divine prerogative as Creator, appointed man (not woman) the 'head.' If women have a problem with that, I suggest they take it up with God because He made the decision. Or, she could choose to not marry.

A BORN LEADER

Leadership, on the other hand, is a matter of personality, temperament, and gifting. The dominant leadership personality in the home can be the man, the woman, or a combination of both. As I described in the Introduction, my wife is a born leader. We call her a natural leader. From the time her feet hit the floor in the morning until she goes to bed at night, she leads. Yet, she has willingly chosen to honor and submit to my headship in our marriage and home under Christ.

SUPPRESS OR RELEASE

Devi leads others naturally and effectively. Therefore, I have only two options. I can either suppress her or release her. Many men try to suppress and control their wives who possess gifts of leadership. They do it out of insecurity, or they lack understanding concerning the marriage roles. They prevent their wives' leadership skills from being released and may even refuse to give their wife a voice in the marriage or allow her the freedom to express herself. What a shame! Often, the wives have superior leadership skills that would serve husbands well in their own growth, if only they would allow their wives the freedom to express their gifts.

Unfortunately, even if a husband tries to suppress his wife's personality, it won't work. She can cover it, mask it, and submit to him, but she can never change who she is any more than you can change your own personality. Furthermore, God doesn't want her to change. He wants her to be herself— the unique woman He created. He wants the man to appreciate his wife's leadership gifts and release them.

Our friends, Anna and Richmond McCoy, both have strong leadership personalities. They have a great concept, which they call the "Increase Decrease Principle." They have chosen to take their cues from John the Baptist, who had to decrease so that Jesus could increase (John 3:30). They both choose to honor each other by knowing when it's time to decrease so that their partner can increase. It's a decision that should come quite naturally for two people committed to each other in love. No special manuals or directions needed. Each one should know instinctively. Depending on the circumstances, one should know when to increase or to decrease. Paul instructs us to do this in the following scriptures:

> *Do nothing out of rivalry or conceit, but in humility count others more significant than yourselves.* Philippians 2:3

> *(Walk) with all humility and gentleness, with patience, bearing with one another in love, eager to maintain the unity of the Spirit in the bond of peace.* Ephesians 4:2-3

HEADSHIP VERSUS LEADERSHIP

For clarity, let's summarize the differences between headship and leadership in marriage:

+ Headship responsibility falls solely on the man.
+ Headship provides the covering for the wife's leadership skills.
+ Headship requires the man to understand that he himself is under the headship of Christ.
+ Headship in marriage should replicate the headship of Christ.
+ The head understands that the buck stops with him.
+ The head oversees the entire home and marriage.
+ The head is the final arbiter in deciding direction for the family.
+ The head is the final point of authority in the home.

On the other hand:

+ Leadership is a natural gift to influence people.
+ Leadership is closely connected to abilities and personality.
+ Leadership can be a combination of skills from the husband and the wife.
+ Leadership can be predominant in one of the spouses.
+ Leadership must be recognized and released by the head of the home (the man) to be effective.

+ Leadership responsibilities can be recognized and released in children when they reach maturity.

LET HER FLY

Now, sir, you must ask yourself the most important question, "In what areas have I refused my wife the freedom to exercise her leadership?" Wisely confess those areas in which you have suppressed her leadership so that she can be fully released to fulfill her calling in God under your headship.

The greatest joy for me, a husband, is to see my wife released and fully functioning in her gifts, personality and calling. If that requires that I decrease in some areas, so that she might increase, so be it. I am the only one who can give my wife wings to soar.

1

[SHE Says]
○○

HEADSHIP AND LEADERSHIP
By: Devi

LARRY ADDRESSES HEADSHIP and leadership in marriage from a male perspective. I fully agree with his presentation of this vital understanding. I believe that the common misunderstanding of headship and leadership causes great confusion in organizations, churches, and especially families.

Larry makes it very clear that headship and leadership are not synonymous. Neither are they gender assigned except in marriage where God ordains that man is the head of his wife. Too often, we use the terms headship and leadership interchangeably. This careless use of two very important, but different, principles confuses the roles and responses of those involved. Maybe I can help to further clarify and elaborate.

HEADSHIP

Headship is assigned authority. The head sits above all positions of leadership. Yet, the head may not have the gift of leadership. Several tiers of leadership may exist under the head. However, headship, unlike leadership, has only one tier. There remains only one head. Let's quickly review the attributes of headship:

+ Heads are the authority.
+ Heads oversee.
+ Heads release leaders to work under them.
+ Heads should be team builders.
+ Heads can be male or female except in marriage where, according to biblical standards, the man is the head.
+ Headship has boundaries.

Let me illustrate headship with the following scenario. If a highway patrolman stops you and writes you a citation for driving too fast, you must submit to him or her. If you don't, you will certainly receive a penalty. Why? Highway patrolmen have assigned authority legitimatized by our laws. The fact that they now gain headship over you does not mean they lead you, nor does it prove that they are good leaders.

You may be a very influential leader in your own workplace. You may command the respect of thousands in your company. Perhaps you even work as CEO. However, the moment those blinking lights turn on, you no longer remain the one in charge. Your authority as CEO does not extend to this situation. When the patrolman stops you, he becomes the head. Who is the leader? You remain a leader, but not his leader.

You must not say to him, "Officer, I possess excellent leadership skills and you do not. So, I must not have to pay this ticket." Neither should you say, "Well, I'll pay the ticket if you will begin leading." No! You submit to his headship and do what he says. After he is gone, you continue in your previous role. You can return to your place of employment as CEO and continue leading and directing those under you.

LEADERSHIP

Unlike headship, leadership has multiple facets:

+ Leadership has various styles.
+ Leadership can be learned.
+ Leadership comes naturally to some and unnaturally to others, depending on their personalities.
+ Leaders have followers.
+ Leaders influence others.
+ Leaders instruct.
+ Leaders delegate.
+ Leaders respect those they influence.

HEADSHIP AND LEADERSHIP IN MARRIAGE

What about the case of a woman with a leadership gift who marries a man without natural leadership ability? This all too familiar scenario often leads to marital difficulties. Sometimes, troubles arise when a wife attempts to coerce her husband into doing what is not natural to him, wanting him to take a leadership role for which he is not equipped. Sometimes, the husband misunderstands his role as the head, thinking that he must dominate and control.

Such marriages will become healthy when both husband and wife understand headship and leadership. The husband must understand that he has been assigned biblical responsibility to oversee his wife. However, he needs to oversee with sensitivity. He needs to release her to serve their family with her leadership skills. He must not feel inadequate or threatened by her natural leadership abilities. His initiative in his headship causes her to respond with her leadership under his headship. His headship releases a new kind of leadership. His leadership and her leadership.

Wives, who possess leadership qualities, must remain careful to not instruct their husbands, continually teaching them and telling them what to do. If a wife has headship authority at her place of employment, she must stay conscious of her need to remove her "boss" hat as she pulls up to her driveway at home. She must enter her home with a servant's attitude. She should use her leadership skills to train her children in responsibility, but she cannot act similarly toward her husband. As she submits to his headship and honors him as her head, she will promote peace in her home and in all of the family relationships.

HEADSHIP AND LEADERSHIP AT WORK

What about a work situation where a woman serves as the boss? This scenario has implications for both the boss and for the men who work under her headship. Men should still treat the boss like a lady, not like another one of the guys. In a professional setting, a man should still give up his seat, rise when she enters a room or approaches a table, and assist her with his masculine strength considering her as the weaker vessel. However, he must remember that weaker does not mean less intelligent!

In the same way, women with headship authority should relate to the men working under her headship with good manners, gracious conduct, respectful behavior and feminine softness. Remember, women, you never have to prove yourselves.

I AM A LEADER!

I am a woman, and I am a natural leader. My mother tells a story from my early days in kindergarten. While at recess one afternoon, I persuaded my classmates to form three even lines. At my command, one line went to the swings, another line went to the teeter-totters and another went to the monkey bars. At my command again, each group changed positions. Amazingly, the kids really did what I told them to do! Remember, leaders have followers—I had followers at the age of five.

Who created me this way? God did. And did He also make me a woman? Of course! So, is it OK for me to lead? Yes! However, because I am a woman and understand headship, I need to honor and respect men, even if I have authority over them.

WHAT ABOUT SUBMISSION?

Don't misunderstand my position in this chapter. I am not addressing this topic to defend myself as a leader, nor am I trying to discredit the importance of submission. Submission remains important in marriage, in corporate relationships, and in every other arena. I fully understand that the principle of authority and functioning with right relationships to authority proves vital to good character. Proper submission to authority is not only biblical, but also releasing to the lives of those who choose to submit. We will discuss submission more fully in a later chapter.

WALKING IN THE SPIRIT

Paul's instructions to the Galatians provide insight on this subject:

> But I say, walk by the Spirit, and you will not gratify the desires of the flesh. Galatians 5:16

> But the fruit of the Spirit is love, joy, peace, patience, kindness, goodness, faithfulness, gentleness, self-control... Galatians 5:22-23

No leader, whether male or female, should relate to another person in a condescending or overbearing manner. Good manners, gentleness and kindness should always prevail. Whether a head, a leader, or both, remember to consider others more important than yourself. In this way, when you as leaders live together, you will double your blessings.

2

[HE Says]

◐

EMBRACE YOUR DIVERSITY

By: Larry

WE READ IN Genesis of how God performs the first surgery among humans— He takes a rib from the side of Adam and creates Eve. This event, in the Garden of Eden, marks the beginning point of when man comes to realize woman's differences.

I wonder if Adam looked at Eve shortly after coming out of anesthesia and said, "Wow, she sure doesn't look like me. I wonder if there are any other areas where we're different." Are you kidding me? Man, was he in for a surprise. Adam and Eve were so opposite you would have thought that they came from different planets. I can also imagine that shortly after they let him out of post-op, he began to complain, "God, did you have to make her so different? We're nothing alike."

Not much has changed since the garden. We still hear men complain that women are different. Duh! Obviously! God purposed it that way! We learn that God intends for Eve to be related to Adam, but totally different from him. Men, your rib is no longer in your side, but it sits across the table looking at you.

Occasionally, I will hear someone say, "You need to get in touch with your feminine side." My retort is simple: "I married my feminine side. Her name is Devi." If you want to get in touch with your feminine side, reach across the table and hold her hand. And by the way, just because you're a creative man doesn't mean that you have a feminine side to you. God surgically removed your feminine side. It merely means that you're a creative man.

I'm going to take a wild guess—I can nearly guarantee that your wife is opposite of you, right? Not just in some things, but everything. She hears things differently than you. She responds differently than you. She processes things differently than you. And, praise God, she looks differently than you. So, what is it that you're complaining about? The question is not, is my wife

9

different than me, but do I appreciate the differences? Beyond that, do I actively resolve to use those differences to produce harmony and unity in my marriage?

I know that it will come as a shock to hear that Devi and I are polar opposites, yet we function in perfect harmony. I process things very slowly; she processes them instantly. I like instant gratification; she likes to plan, save, and wait. She moves very, very fast, and I move very, very, very slowly. She loves social situations; I love solitude. She loves to talk; I love to read. She loves to garden; I love to sit in gardens. She loves to cook; I love to eat. She loves gourmet; I love McDonalds. She loves serious, suspense-filled movies; I like comedies. Devi loves to speak to the crowds; I love to spend one-on-one time with people. She loves to shop, and I love to do anything in the world *but* shop. I would rather hang-glide upside down than shop.

So now, go ahead and think about some of the ways in which you are opposite of your spouse. The question is, do you appreciate her diversity or despise it? You cannot come into unity without diversity. Let me say it again; you cannot come into unity without diversity. Sameness never produces unity, only diversity does. You cannot become united with yourself. God didn't create you to be a soloist; He desires for you and your wife to harmonize, to "sing a duet" throughout your day to day life.

GOD CREATED ONE PERSON

I started learning about diversity over forty-eight years ago, when, on our honeymoon, Devi and I drove around to find a parking space. My bride of one day instantly spotted a parking space and pointed it out. Of course, it was in a different location than the one that I, with my ultimate reasoning, had already decided upon. Since then, not a single day has gone by that I haven't zigged when she zagged, gone left when she went right, or said "no" when she said "yes." Decisions and ideas that seem totally logical to me can seem completely illogical to her, and vice versa. I stand in amazement at our differences. I sometimes wonder, "How could one so beautiful be wrong so often?" No, actually that's not true. What I am constantly amazed at is how much we work in harmony, joining our diversity together into one, much stronger position.

You may notice, by a careful reading of the second chapter of Genesis, that God didn't create two people. He created only one. He just made two people out of the one creation. So in reality, everything that the man does or says is only half the answer. The other half of the answer lies with the person who makes up the other half of him.

Let me say it again; you cannot come into
unity without diversity.

God's grand design calls for two totally different people, male and female, to come together in the covenant of marriage and unite together as one. It takes the two opposite opinions and viewpoints to come to the best decisions.

OPPOSITES ATTRACT OR DO THEY?

Isn't it interesting that before a couple marries, they are attracted to each other because of their differences? Then as soon as they say, "I do," the differences become irritating. What used to be cute is now annoying. A truism, namely "opposites attract," changes after marriage to "opposites repel."

It used to be so cute when Devi would leave her shoes scattered all over the floor. But, there came a day when it wasn't. I remember the night when the scattered shoes landed on the floor on my side of the bed, but I didn't notice it until I got up in the middle of the night and tripped over them.

Before we were married, Devi's strong leadership personality was so appealing to me. After we were married, what used to be her positive leadership skills turned into, she's just plain bossy. But did she really change or was I viewing her from a different perspective?

I have a theory. I believe that traits that were cute before marriage will often become contemptible after marriage. However, a healthy marriage must return to that cute stage.

For instance, Devi's aggressive leadership style that I found attractive in my pre-marriage experience must return to that state of cuteness. Does that make sense?

What I found so appealing about her spontaneous way of walking out of her shoes, as soon as she walks in the door, had to return to the same pre-marriage cuteness that attracted me to her in the first place.

What are those things in your spouse that have gone from cute to contemptible? Unless you return them to the same "cuteness" that attracted you in the first place, your marriage will remain unhealthy and the gulf between the two of you will widen.

God has not called us to change the personality of our spouses. After marriage, we often feel that God endows us with the "gift of criticism," so we can actively change the things we don't like about our partners. Well, I've got news for you. He doesn't. God wants us to appreciate our spouses' differences in style and personality, rather than attempt to conform them to our own

11

images. God creates us in His image. Then, He puts us together and says, "Learn to work together. Each of you has the perfect ingredient to complement the other."

GOD LIKES SYMPHONY

We find one of the most powerful scriptures in the entire Word of God in the book of Matthew:

Again I say to you, if two of you agree on earth about anything they ask, it will be done for them by my Father in heaven. Matthew 18:19

The word "agree" comes from the same Greek word from which we derive our English word "symphony." Jesus says that if two people will begin to harmonize, God will do anything for them that they ask. God always listens to the sounds of harmony. He's not looking for solos, either by the man or the woman. Solos are dead, hollow and unappealing without background music to accompany them. Whether it's voices or instruments, music sounds better when diverse tones unify for a purposed outcome. Marriages, too often, consist of one of the partners working totally alone without the compliment of the other's contribution.

Even God works in harmony and symphony with the Son and Holy Spirit. Nothing happens without the cooperation of the others. God sets the entire universe to work in symphony as well. The universe works as a synergism in which the co-operation of every created thing is necessary. This being true, how much more must husband and wife, the crowning point of God's creation, work together? Marriage partners must learn to harmonize. Remember, God listens. Until He hears a symphony, He remains under no obligation to answer prayers (See I Peter 3:7).

IT'S HARMONY

In the Bible, God created the entire universe, from the heavens to the animals, by His voice. "And God said," His spoken word was all that was needed to bring something out of nothing. However, when God created man, He did more than just speak him into existence. He came to earth and personally formed him out of the dust of the ground. God then breathed His own breath into Adam. Man is God's creative energy at its best. He not only created man, but He created him in His own image. Following that act of creation, He took the woman out of the man. Then He brought the two back together and told them to become one. Biblical unity is not "oneness;" it's "harmony." It's two people bringing their differing talents, opinions and insights together for the common good. Remember, unity is not an option; God commands it.

In God's divine economy and wisdom, He chooses to bring opposites together. Consequently, their choice to unify leads to a more complete, healthy and whole relationship. Praise God that opposites attract. If you and your spouse did not have unique personalities and different backgrounds, your decisions would have no balance, safety, wisdom, protection or ultimate success. It's diversity that allows for effectiveness.

PRAISE GOD FOR YOUR DIFFERENCES

This is a good time to stop and reflect on, maybe even write down, the areas in which you and your spouse differ. Then after listing them, take time to praise God for your differences.

For example, a man might say of his wife:

+ She's emotional, and I'm rational.
+ She's practical, and I'm visionary.
+ She's multi-tasked, and I'm single-tasked.
+ She's outgoing, and I'm introverted.
+ She's quiet, and I'm extroverted.
+ She's socially energized, and I have few social needs.

A woman might say:

+ He's content to stay at home, while I want to socialize.
+ He's prone to make snap decisions when purchasing things, while I want to take time to compare prices and think it through.
+ He's content to watch television, when I want to do projects.
+ He's quick to offer solutions, when I want to talk about the problem.
+ He's suspicious of people, while I'm more trusting.
+ He's slow at reaching conclusions, while I can process them quickly.

+ He always wants to play and I'm always trying to get him to work.

It's time to verbally praise God for your differences. Spouses need to work to compliment rather than oppose each other. What you view as obstacles, you can find to be assets. Only when we bring our diverse viewpoints, insights, opinions and observations together do we become valuable to each other and to the Kingdom of God. Most importantly, what one spouse lacks, the other is likely to possess. Doesn't that seem logical? If God removed part of your personality at creation, it is only restored through marriage. No longer view each other's differing viewpoints as negative. They are extremely positive and necessary for both of you to succeed.

I often hear couples say, "I can't let her (or him) know she's right or she'll think she's won." Won what? Is this a battle? Do you think your spouse is your enemy? Spouses do not fight on opposite sides. This is not a war. You're on the same side. Any victory for her is a victory for you. Who cares which one is right when the rightness of one automatically makes it right for the other?

MARRIAGE AND THE BODY OF CHRIST

Therefore a man shall leave his father and mother and hold fast to his wife, and the two shall become one flesh. This mystery is profound, and I am saying that it refers to Christ and the church. Ephesians 5:31-32

Marriage replicates the Body of Christ—many members operate under one Head for the purpose of accomplishing God's purpose on earth. Diversity is as important in the marriage as it is in the Body of Christ. Learn to appreciate your differences rather than despise them. Make a symphony. Two are much better than one when they learn to harmonize.

Two are better than one, because they have a good reward for their toil. For if they fall, one will lift up his fellow. But woe to him who is alone when he falls and has not another to lift him up! Ecclesiastes 4:9-10

The more the two of you work in harmony, the healthier your marriage will be; and the healthier your marriage is, the healthier the Body of Christ will be.

Everything depends on unity and unity cannot be achieved without harmony. It's time that we men stop singing solos and start harmoniously singing duets. After harmony, we can work on the symphony, that's when the kids come along and add their diversity to the mix.

2

[SHE Says]

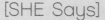

EMBRACE YOUR DIVERSITY
By: Devi

LARRY ZIGS AND I zag, so he says. Don't confuse this with Larry thinks he is right and I think he is wrong. Zigging and zagging have nothing to do with right or wrong. When I sew and set the zigzag stitch on the machine, I do this for one reason—to prevent the seam from unraveling. The harmonizing of our diverse viewpoints strengthens our decisions. It enlarges our personal perspectives and unifies our ultimate direction.

Webster defines the word *diverse* in this way: "Two or more things markedly different from one another." This is not a surprise to anyone who understands the male and female species. From the beginning, humans were designed by God in a very different way for very different purposes.

For man and woman to be the same was never in God's plan. The second chapter of Genesis records the diverse methods that God used to create man and woman. God made man from the dust of the earth and He formed woman from the rib and flesh of man. Man was created to "work and keep" the garden of Eden and woman was created to be his "helper." Man is the stronger and woman is the weaker in our body structures. We are diverse in every way. Our physical structure is different, our emotional capacity is different and even our spiritual sensitivities are different. Man is the giver of life through his seed and woman is the carrier of life through her womb. Nothing about a man and a woman are the same. There is no such thing as unisex in God's creation--to cross pollinate our diversity is to multiply a new unique generation of diverse people. It is an amazing system created by God and certainly one to be appreciated and celebrated.

So, why is it that we try to convert our spouse to be like us? The lack of appreciation of diversity is the core reason for most couple's points of disagreements. Arguments are merely discussions from two different people who attempt to convert the other's opinions, behaviors, habits and preferences to their own. One who argues their own points of view, coercing others to be like them, are people who consider themselves personally superior and refuse to appreciate and embrace diversity of thought.

It is absolutely impossible to change your mate to be like you so don't even try. It is better to look at your differences with an endearing eye and be grateful for them.

Larry says that when my feet hit the floor in the morning, the first sounds he hears are pitter-patters in a fast pace. He thinks I have only one pace—fast. Together, we are the typical example of the tortoise and the hare. While the hare runs fast, gets tired, and sleeps beside the road, the slow tortoise paces himself and wins the race. If Larry conformed to me and rushed around, becoming anxious and frenzied, we would never accomplish our combined tasks. Neither would he have the motivation to begin a great mission without my jumping up and getting us started. The truth is: we need the diversity of one another to reach our combined goals.

> It is absolutely impossible to change your mate to be like you so don't even try.

A SPOUSE IN MY OWN IMAGE? NO THANKS!

Larry is right! Diversity is good! I don't even like being with people who are just like me. They exhaust me. I know what they are going to say before they say it. Larry, on the other hand, still keeps me guessing even after forty-eight years of marriage. I have never figured him out, and I hope I never do.

I love listening to him. I always want to know what he thinks. In fact, it fascinates me to understand that he "thinks" before he speaks. Me? I speak and then think about what I just said. Sometimes, after I have really thought about it, I realize that I don't even believe what I just said!

> We need the diversity of one another to reach our combined goals.

I love the silent times we spend together. We can sit in the same room and say nothing. At least, he says nothing. I usually break the silence. He smiles at me with adoring eyes.

We spend a lot of time together on airplanes and we both like to read. However, I always read my favorite phrases and sentences aloud for him to hear, hoping he will be equally impressed with the profundity of my author.

He smiles at me with a crooked smile (A crooked smile is Larry's kind way to say, "I'm not enjoying what you are trying to get me to do").

Larry is my rest and I am his energy.

Please don't try to change your spouse into your image. If you do, you will not like them or yourself. Your marriage is meant to create a duet sung in beautiful harmony. If you have coerced or persuaded your mate into being like you, your mutual songs are all in unison—that's boring. They may even be badly out of tune! The bottom line is you need the uniqueness of each other.

Enjoy your differences. Our relationship is filled with laughter and most of the time we are laughing at our differences. Learn to laugh at yourself and with your spouse; never laugh at your spouse. Larry is my rest and I am his energy. Both are equally necessary for good health. We have a healthy marriage because with his zig and my zag, nothing can tear us apart.

3

[HE Says]
◐

CONTROLLERS OR RELEASERS
By: Larry

F OR THE SAKE of simplicity, I'll put all men in the category of either Releasers or Controllers. Obviously, that is much too general and simplistic. Many men are controlling in some areas and releasers in others. However, I will present the extremes for the sake of emphasis. Let's look first at Controllers.

CONTROLLERS

Controllers: Hearty, heady, heavy-handed, half-witted, harebrained, hard-mouthed, hard-nosed, hapless, hopeless, hoggish, hairless hominids, with fewer guts than common houseflies. Men in this category feel that the only way to maintain their dominance is to control and suppress their wives. Needless to say, I will not be sending these men Christmas cards this year because I feel they are absolutely dangerous. How dare they take the beautiful gifts that God gives them in their wives and keep them suppressed for the sake of inflating their own egos and stroking their machismo? This form of masculine pride needs to be flushed down the porcelain facility. It is not biblical.

Controllers lead with anger, intimidation, manipulation, suppression and force. They lead, all right, but it's negative and destructive. People follow them out of fear rather than out of respect. Controllers turn their beautiful wives into cringing, fawning, cowering, fearful objects of darkness—slaves to a beastly husband. Through the years, you will notice their wives' light filled countenances slowly become sullen, silenced, drawn, and darkened until they give up all hope. The light of their lovely personalities gradually becomes dimmer until it finally extinguishes. I would not want to stand in such a man's shoes on judgment day when he has to give account to God for abusing his authority.

I've personally known and observed once beautiful women become hardly recognizable because of insecure, heavy-handed husbands. If you're one of these men, you need to repent to your wife, to Jesus, to your children, to your employees, and anyone else you've manhandled. You might need to take your repentance all the way to the President in the Oval Office just to make sure it's cleaned out of your system.

If people follow you for any reason other than the good, godly example you set for them, then you're out of sync with the Holy Spirit and the entire Word of God. Your goal should be for people to <u>want</u> (not <u>have</u>) to follow you. Submission should always be subjective, because the person under your leadership understands the biblical principle involved. One should not coerce or cajole another into obedience. Your wife should never feel forced into submission through tyranny. If you force her to submit, you violate the entire Word of God. Her submission must come from her own volition.

Much of what we view as 'rebellion' in a woman is nothing more than resistance to the control and manipulation of an insecure man. Such a man fears what his wife might become if he loses control. In addition, a controlling man may act out in anger and frustration when people, especially his wife, don't conform to his repressive agenda. It angers him when things and people don't line up to his demands. In an insecure man's army, he is the general and everyone else, especially his wife, are the privates.

Once again, I admit that this is simplistic, but I believe that a control issue equals a pride issue—male pride in its most deadly form. Though he's an adult, he still plays the childhood game of "King of the Mountain." He's King and he owns the mountain.

RELEASERS

Men, your calling is not to control your wife, but to release her. Release her to become all God created her to be. Don't fear that she will become better than you. Praise God if she does. Don't worry that she will gain more attention or notoriety than you. Praise God if she does. Don't be afraid that she will make more money than you. Praise God for His blessing to both of you!

Your wife cannot excel without it bringing honor to you. She reflects you. If she shines, it's because she's catching the glow from you. First Corinthians 11:7 states that the woman is the glory of the man. If you radiate, she will radiant. If you become clouded by your distorted, controlling spirit, she cannot properly reflect you without uncovering your darkness. When you shine, it will immediately show in her countenance. If you want to know what the husband truly looks like as a man, look in the mirror at his wife's face. That will tell you volumes.

The opposite of the controlling husband is the releasing husband. You can't have it both ways. You're either a Controller or a Releaser. So, ask yourself the obvious question: which one are you? If I've described you in the first several paragraphs, then it's time to change. Do you want to imitate Christ?

> If you want to know what the husband truly looks like as a man, look in the mirror at his wife's face.

How Did Jesus Do It?

We read in the New Testament about how Jesus took twelve common men and, except for Judas, made every one of them uncommon. These eleven uneducated followers of Christ turned the world upside down—or maybe I should say right side up. How did He do it?

1. *He believed in them.*

   The disciples knew that Jesus was <u>for</u> them, not against them. They had no doubts. They would follow their Lord to the ends of the earth because of His commitment to them. It's true that believing in other people expresses love, but it's more than that. It tells them in no uncertain terms that you support them, you stand with them, and you remain committed to their successes.

2. *He gave them His authority.*

   Every time Jesus sent the disciples out with the Kingdom message, He gave them the authority to replicate what they had seen Him do. Some men fear that their wives might excel beyond their own successes. Jesus evidently did not fear that possibility. In fact, in John 14:12-14, He promised that His disciples would do even greater works than those He had accomplished. Jesus had no fear of being upstaged by their successes. His final words to the disciples in Matthew 28:18-19 indicated that they were to possess the same authority that the Father had given Him.

21

3. *He allowed them to fail without berating them.*

Not one of the disciples made it through the three and a half years of training without having notable failures. Of course, Peter comes immediately to mind, but he is not alone. They all forsook Jesus at His arrest in the Garden of Gethsemane. Not one remained loyal. Yet, the scripture never records Jesus berating, humiliating, or speaking abusively to them. In fact, He hosted them for a home cooked breakfast on the shores of Galilee not too many days following their defeat. Jesus honored His disciples when they were at their lowest so He could release them to their highest potential.

4. *He loved them with unqualified love.*

God's love is always unqualified. You don't have to earn it. People cannot be truly secure unless they have an environment of unqualified love in which to live and excel. If you want your spouse to live securely, released, fulfilled and joyful, give her unqualified love. Love her, says Paul in Ephesians 5:25, the way that Christ loved the church—a love that took Him to the cross, and a love that willingly laid down His life for her so that she might live.

5. *He left His glory with them when He returned to the Father.*

A releasing husband makes plans for the future of his wife in the event of his death. He wants her to remain cared for, blessed, comfortable, and enjoying the fruits of their labor together even after he passes away and can no longer care for her himself. Before His death, Jesus prayed that the Father would give the disciples the same glory that He had with the Father before the creation of the world. Every blessing that God has given you must be passed on to your wife and posterity. Don't stop the glory. Don't stop the blessing. Don't begrudge your wife what is rightfully hers. Leave an inheritance to your wife that shows you cared enough for her to ensure her security after your death.

6. *He prayed for them.*

In His final prayer, Jesus spoke to the Father concerning His disciples. Jesus desired that they have His glory, His unity, and His Father's protection. Prayer for your wife deposits an irreplaceable blessing into her life. According to God's Word, you are the head of your wife. Your prayers furnish your wife with an impenetrable shield of faith that provides for her protection, blessing, anointing, and release. The greatest gift you can ever give your wife is your devoted, daily prayer on her behalf.

7. *He called out the potential in them.*

Jesus saw His disciples for what they would become, not what they were. He changed Simon's name to Peter, knowing that someday Peter would become a rock. As one person has said, "In the presence of sinners, Jesus dreamed of saints." He concentrated not on their weaknesses, but on their strengths. Jesus had faith that His disciples would fulfill their greatest potential. He saw the finished vessel when it was still a lump of clay. He encouraged them with heartening words such as, "Go for it. You can do it!" A husband who is a Releaser will give confidence to his wife that she can do anything. He sees what God intended for her to become, and lends the weight of his confidence in her until it becomes reality.

8. *He led them by example.*

Jesus did not lead by coercion and intimidation. His followers saw Him pray. They witnessed His miracles. They saw Him love the unlovely. They saw Christ live a life of purity, sincerity and truth. He was touchable, compassionate and warm, not distant or aloof. Jesus loved children and taught His followers to love children. He loved sinners and encouraged them to do the same.

He was meek, but not soft. He had authority, but never abused it. He earned respect rather than demanding it. He relied totally on the Father for direction. He put the Father's will foremost and sought to do only those things that brought glory to the Father. He was driven not by the people's needs, but by the Father's direction. Most of all, Jesus was completely obedient to the will of the Father.

A husband who is a Releaser will give confidence to his wife that she can do anything.

9. *He served them.*

Jesus didn't put on the garments of a servant and wash the disciples' feet at the last supper in order to impress His followers. It wasn't a theatrical stunt. It showed His character and who He really was. True leadership, Jesus' style, always results from you serving your way into it. Promotion in Christ does not come from elevating yourself, but from kneeling down. Serving should not be the "love language" of a few men who know no other way in which to express their love, but an active part of every man's life. When you arrive home from work at night, don your serving clothes. It's time to serve, not recline in front of the television while your wife and children cater to your whims and the dog delivers your paper. You serve them first, and then they can reverse the process as they follow your example.

10. *He gave them gifts.*

In addition to breathing on the disciples in the Upper Room on resurrection night, Jesus also poured out the Father's promise of the Holy Spirit on the Day of Pentecost. Jesus had hardly departed into the heavens and seated Himself at the Father's right hand when the gifts began to arrive. Men quite often fail to understand a woman's need for gifts. Unless she drops a multitude of hints prior to a birthday or anniversary, the possibility remains that the special day will slip away without her receiving any token of his affection. Where are the gifts, men? It's less important *what* they are than *that* they are! To a woman, gifts mean sensitivity, love and thoughtfulness. Because *"Every good gift and every perfect gift is from above, coming down from the Father . . ."* (James 1:17), you become an extension of the Father's beneficence when you give.

11. *He was gentle with them.*

Jesus knew how to treat women. He possessed a humble and meek spirit. Matthew 12 quotes Isaiah's description of Jesus as one who never argued or raised the volume of His voice in the streets. He was so gentle that He refused to break a bent reed or snuff out a smoking wick. Jesus characterized the word "gentleman"— a gentle man. A real man is not braggadocios, bombastic, loud, insensitive, or full of arrogant bravado. He is gentle. He leads with gentleness, not force. He doesn't need volume or anger to enforce his leadership. He's not afraid that others might misconstrue his sensitivity as weakness because he's secure with his identity in Christ.

LET'S FOLLOW THE MASTER RELEASER!

Men, the way Jesus brought these failed fisherman and their cohorts into release is the same way you can bring release to your wife and others that you lead. You're either a Controller or a Releaser. Make your decision today. Who have you been in the past, and who do you want to be in the future? As soon as God sees your heart and witnesses your desire to change, He will help you do the rest. Let's get started! I'm behind you!

3

◯◖

CONTROLLER OR RELEASER
By Devi

L ARRY WRITES TO men almost as if women do not need to take inventory. But I want to address the same question to women. Are you a Controller or a Releaser? Do you need to direct, dictate, dominate, disagree, disarm, and disengage the decisions or should I say, the attempted decisions of your husband? When he gives direction about simple things such as: where to eat, what to do, or what to wear, do you usually make alternate suggestions? Do you subtly think that you have better ideas than him?

FLAWED FEMINISM

The feminist philosophy has radically affected women's thoughts about men. Feminism pledges to give us freedom and fulfillment, but these promised benefits have yet to come to pass. Rather, this independent, self-indulgent way of thinking leads us to habits that destroy the very character of healthy, gratifying relationships. We learn to think, "If I don't take care of myself, nobody will." In terms of assuming personal responsibility, this statement is valid. However, this attitude extends way beyond personal responsibility. It is a mind-set of self-protection, self-exaltation, self-gratification and self-centered living.

The feminist platform began with a desire for women to have equal rights. However, that worthy desire has carried us to the opposite extreme of women wanting to dominate men. Equality doesn't seem to suffice. Early in the movement, feminist leaders sponsored campaigns insisting that women no longer portray sex. These leaders voiced their opinions very vocally, seeking to change the public image of women. They aspired to influence the media to redress women in "Power" suits.

Recently, while I was traveling, a young professional woman sat beside me on the airplane. She began leafing through the pages of the several magazines that she had brought on board. I could tell this was not recreational reading, but that somehow these magazine pages related to her profession. She hesitated at an advertisement and studied it carefully. The captivating model on the page wore a scanty outfit and posed seductively. I intruded on her deep thought with this question, "Where are our feminist leaders now? Earlier in the movement, they spoke against women being used in this way, insisting that females maintain a public image of professionalism and power." Her response horrified me. She deliberately looked at me, pressed her index finger onto the page and said, "This is power."

I sat speechless. I had nothing more to say. My mind raced, remembering stories of women sitting in my office, devastated because of their husbands' addictions to pornography. She spoke accurately. Feminists no longer lobby for the professional image of women; they are content to control men, regardless of how it is done. Advertisers know this and use the power of women's exposed bodies to ensnare men.

SELF-SERVING

Women's magazines now carry titles such as *SELF* and *ME*. These titles enforce the "Me first" mentality. Such attitudes put all others in second positions. This way of thinking keeps us from considering others more important than ourselves (Philippians 2:3). You cannot honor your spouse unless you willfully let him be first. I'm amazed at the effectiveness of the "Golden Rule" when practiced in relationships:

> *And as you wish that others would do to you, do so to them.*
> Luke 6:31

In other words, treat others how you want them to treat you. It really works! Women usually control by manipulation and seduction. We expertly maneuver circumstances, situations, and conversations in such a way that we can determine our preferred outcome. We barter and seduce, saying, "If you'll do this, I'll do that." Women need to become aware of the powerful, but sometimes subtle, force they wield. They can take control without really knowing it.

Controlling does not make you happy. In fact, after you successfully take control and your husband allows you to make all decisions, you will soon feel exhausted, emotionally tired, and internally resentful that he is not leading. You get what you want, but soon, you don't want what you got. If this is the case, you may want to turn things around. You might ask, "Where do I begin?" or "How do I become a releaser rather than a controller?"

THINK THESE THOUGHTS

Start by changing your mind. Change the way you think. Think on positive things and follow the instructions of Paul:

> *Finally, brothers, whatever is true, whatever is honorable, whatever is just, whatever is pure, whatever is lovely, whatever is commendable, if there is any excellence, if there is anything worthy of praise, think about these things.* Philippians 4:8

You get what you want, but soon, you don't want what you got.

Make a list of your husband's positive attributes. The lawn may look like a cow pasture before he gets around to mowing it. But rather than focusing on this, think of other things that he does really well. Write them down as a reminder and place these things first in your mind.

Your thoughts become your words—your words become your actions—your actions become your habits—your habits make up your character—your character determines your destiny. Wow! It's no wonder that the wisdom of Scripture tells us to fix our minds on the best attributes of others.

RELEASE HIM WITH PRAISE

Speak words of affirmation, confidence, hope, and possibility to your husband. Believe in him. Learn about the things he likes and participate in things that are important to him. Do not belittle him.

You have the power to make him a king and be his crown, or you can undermine his character by shaming him. Solomon says it this way:

> *An excellent wife is the crown of her husband, but she who brings shame is like rottenness in his bones.* Proverbs 12:4

TAKE ACTION

Physically affirm him. If he loses his hair, talk about how handsome you think bald men are. If he lacks muscle, tell him how much you like slim trim men. Touch him. Stroke him. Create a new habit of connecting. Kiss and hug him at least ten times per day. When you enter and exit his presence, speak to him. Wink at him from across a room.

Larry and I can be on opposite sides of a large auditorium. Perhaps he approaches the platform to speak. He will look for me and allow his eyes to meet mine. I smile. My smile says, "I believe in you. I'm praying for you. I'm proud to be your wife."

Not long ago, Larry preached as a guest speaker on Father's Day at a very large church in Southern California. I spoke at the Sunday evening service on the same day. When I approached the platform, I glanced at him. He winked. That was all I needed. His wink affirmed me, supported me, believed in me, and released me to be my best for that congregation.

Your supportive thoughts, words, actions and habits can create a foundation of relational character in you that can stand the test of time. You may even notice your husband's weakness increasing and yet, it won't bother you as much.

RELEASE HIM

I appreciate the age-old saying, "Behind every good man is a woman." This saying had to come from somewhere. Most women do not realize or take responsibility for the power that they have over men. Likewise, selfish, controlling women are usually the ones behind men who fail. Men who do not succeed most often have mothers or wives who do not believe in them, touch them, or love them.

Fear often prohibits women from releasing their husbands. The truth is, you cannot control and release at the same time. So what do you fear? Is it a concern about security that fuels your fear? Do you think that if you trust your husband, he will not do what is best for you and for your family? Do you not want to take a risk? Well, I'm here to tell you that releasing your partner does put you at risk, but that's okay. His failure may bring you pain. However, his eventual success will bring you prosperity. Take the risk and you can share in the outcome. All success requires elements of risk. Your refusal to allow him to venture and conquer will kill his initiative and deprive you from sharing in his joy and fulfillment.

Fear not! Turn him loose. Reposition yourself and enjoy the blessings of seeing your husband prosper.

> Your refusal to allow him to venture and conquer will kill his initiative and deprive you from sharing in his joy and fulfillment.

4

[HE Says]

◑

SUBMITTED AND SATISFIED

By Larry

W**E USUALLY ADDRESS** women when we talk about submission. There's a reason for that, and it's not because women rebel more than men. The main reason is that men are usually the ones preaching the sermons on submission. Therefore, it becomes logical that men would want to direct attention away from themselves, right? What male preachers would willingly incriminate themselves? The answer is, "Not many." For the purpose of addressing the unaddressed, I will address this address to the male addressees only. So, women, sit back, enjoy, and gloat if need be. Give a high five to someone nearby, but please don't do any elbowing.

A joke made the rounds of the church circuit several years ago about the man who had heard a teaching on submission for the first time. He learned how his wife should immediately submit to his authority. Delighted, he went home to instruct his wife in this newfound doctrine and to set his marriage in order. After he delivered his jeremiad to his wife, he didn't see her for a while. Then, after about two weeks, he saw her again… out of one eye. Are you laughing? I'm sure all the women said, "Amen!" and the men said, "Oh, me."

BIBLICAL SUBMISSION

The Bible's teaching on submission, unlike most teaching coming from pulpits over the past three decades, is a principle that relates to both men and women because the Bible does tell us to submit to one another.

In order to fully explore the idea of submission, we need to take a look at the opposite of submission—authority. This subject leaks back into the control issue a little bit, but authority is broader than simply being the head of the home while releasing your wife. Let's consider the definition of true biblical authority and identify what authority is not.

Authority can give life or it can devastate one's life. Heavy-handed, unilateral, suppressive and dictatorial authority is evil, non-biblical, and ungodly. Properly exercised authority is a liberating, productive, successful, and highly effective organizational model.

DEMONIC AUTHORITY

The misuse of authority can become demonic. Over the centuries of human civilization, dictators have abused their authority and opened the door for Satan's activity. Please note that what distinguishes Satan's authority from that of the Holy Spirit is his hatred of submission. Satan demands submission from his subjects, but he resists their submission to other authorities, especially the authority of Jesus Christ. The devil knows that biblical authority would also require him to submit to the lordship of Christ.

Satan hates the doctrine of submission. No wonder he stirs up such resistance and opposition when we teach on the subject. Submission is what keeps authority from becoming evil. The devil craves authority, but not submission. Maybe someone should tell Satan and his crowd that they will submit either in this life or the next, but they will eventually submit.

> *Therefore God has highly exalted him and bestowed on him the name that is above every name, so that at the name of Jesus every knee should bow, in heaven and on earth and under the earth, and every tongue confess that Jesus Christ is Lord, to the glory of God the Father.* Philippians 2:9-11

Do you see how important it is for all who exercise authority to be under authority? Jesus had authority because He submitted to the authority of the Father. You have authority because you submit to Jesus and to others who have authority over you. Your wife and children have authority as they submit to your authority.

It is dangerous for a leader to exercise authority without submitting to headship himself. The harness of submission benefits leaders and followers. It creates the brokenness, humility and compassion that produce a good leader. But more importantly, if a leader doesn't maintain submission to a still higher authority, he risks abusing his own authority as well as losing it.

Submission is essential for effective headship. A submitted heart equals an obedient and surrendered heart. Submission that comes from a begrudging subservient attitude to leadership undermines the effectiveness of submission.

This kind of attitude destroys the leader's success. "Oh, I guess I'll submit if I have to," doesn't cut the mustard with your authority, nor does it move the hand of God. God knows your heart and man recognizes your impure motives.

Godly authority, exercised under biblical guidelines, should remain the ultimate goal of all leaders. Every leader must fully submit to those above him. Leaders who do not submit to other leaders will eventually fail.

Submission is God's idea. The word submission is a military term meaning to put yourself under one who has a higher rank than you. The Greek word "hupotasso" comes from the word "hupo," a preposition meaning "under," and "tasso," a verb meaning to "arrange in an orderly fashion." Everyone in God's army must line up under someone. If you're a lieutenant, you line up under a captain. Likewise, captains submit to majors who submit to colonels who submit to generals. We all start out in God's army as privates, and privates submit to everyone! But all must line up before God to honor His authority. God does not move corporately or individually until everyone falls in line and functions in His prescribed position.

Submission is not a gender issue, according to Scripture. All must submit to authority or they cannot have authority. It's a simple rule. Memorize it. You can't be **over** until you're **under.**

- Jesus submitted to His parents. Luke 2:51
- Demons submitted to the disciples. Luke 10:17,20
- Israel sinned by not submitting to the righteousness of God. Romans 10:3
- Believers submit to all forms of authority. Romans 13:1
- The spirits of the prophets submit to the prophets. I Corinthians 14:32
- Believers submit to each other. Ephesians 5:21
- Wives submit to their husbands. Ephesians 5:22; Colossians 3:18; Titus 2
- The Church submits to Christ. Ephesians 5:25
- Servants submit to their masters (Employees to Employers). Titus 2:9
- The whole world submits to Christ. Hebrews 2:5
- Everyone submits to the Father of spirits. Hebrews 12:9
- Believers submit to their spiritual authorities. Hebrews 13:17
- Believers submit to God before resisting the devil. James 4:7

+ All mankind submits to those in authority over them. I Peter 2:13
+ Angels and authorities submit to Christ. I Peter 3:22
+ The younger submit to the older. I Peter 5:5

Submission is not a gender issue.

Submission is God's way of liberating leaders. When leaders do it God's way, they move into a proper and healthy release of authority. More importantly, God chooses this method to align the entire universe under the headship and authority of His Son, Jesus Christ. Submission is God's idea; therefore, it is a great idea. We must embrace it with joy. God does not call us to practice submission in order to make us all miserable. He calls us into submission so that He can release His full authority in us. God uses our submission to set us up for success in our positions of authority.

That leads me to a probing question for husbands, fathers, employers, pastors, and leaders of every kind. Do you personally submit to authority? If not, you remain vulnerable, unprotected and ineffective. Your effectiveness only comes when you're under authority. You have no right to expect submission from those you lead if you do not submit to authority. Too often, husbands demand submission from their wives, yet they do not practice it themselves.

Fortunately, during the formative years of our marriage, God and my wife gave me enough grace until I learned how to correctly exercise authority. It took time, though. I stumbled over people a bit roughshod during the process, injuring my wife, family and congregation at times. I sincerely tried to lead, but I functioned without being under headship. I exercised authority without submitting to authority.

> *Biblical authority never demands, cajoles, suppresses or manipulates people. God-given authority builds people up instead of tearing them down* (2 Corinthians 10:8; 13:10).

My own submission to authority wavered at times in my younger years. At about twelve, I learned an especially valuable lesson on submission. My dad, who had spent nearly all of his adult life working as a foreman for several California vineyards, took an afternoon to plant some grape vines in our back yard. As usual, he recruited me to help him. After digging a hole for the grapevine, he asked me to hand him the grape stake. I had no idea that my reply would have such serious repercussions. "Get it yourself," I said. Without saying a word, Dad laid down the grapevine, walked over to the grape stake and got it himself. Shortly thereafter, I got it. Without warning, my dad lowered the board of education to the seat of understanding and I went flying across the yard. I want you to know that I got it! In more ways than one, I got it. I really understand the meaning of submission. I understand it firsthand. Would you believe that to this day I've never told anyone, "Get it yourself?" With one solid whack of a grape stake, I learned to remember the valuable principle of submission. Blessings come if you submit and penalties come if you don't.

The oft-quoted twenty-second verse of Ephesians five instructs women to submit to their husbands. However, the verse immediately before provides the context for all the marriage scriptures that follow. Paul commands in verse twenty-one to *submit to one another out of reverence to Christ*. Did you get that, men? Before demanding submission from your wife, you need to submit to one another.

> Your submission releases God to bless you.

Devi and I both believe strongly in the principle of submission. She submits to me, and I submit to her. And what determines our submission is not always an issue of who's right. In fact, it rarely is. Neither of us portrays a melancholy hands-on-hip attitude of "Okay, you're right. I'll submit to you." More often than not, we want to honor the other person by foregoing our own desires. I can honor Devi by surrendering my own agenda and pursuing hers. Submission is not a forced give-in to maintain peace, but rather it is a decision to yield to the wisdom of the other. You and your spouse need to understand that your authority as leaders never weakens by submitting to each other. It is, in fact, strengthened.

Without doubt, one of the most poignant stories of submission comes from Jesus' encounter with the Roman centurion, a story found in the Bible in Matthew chapter eight. This centurion has authority over one hundred soldiers, yet he recognizes and submits to the authority of Jesus. The Lord, in turn, makes it very clear to the centurion that because of his willingness to submit to authority, his servant will be healed, his faith will be noted in Israel, and he will be included as a Gentile in the Kingdom of God. That's not a bad reward for doing only one thing, namely submitting to authority. You, too, can receive an equally great reward.

Trust me. No, better yet, trust the Word of God. Your submission releases God to bless you.

4

[SHE Says]

◖◗

SUBMITTED AND SATISFIED

By: Devi

I T PUZZLES ME that people have such difficulty embracing the concept of submission—such difficulty that they rarely address the topic in a direct way. Maybe it's because I grew up in a household where my mother respected my father. Now, do not misunderstand and think that my spunky mother behaved passively and permissively, as a needy woman who never asserted herself. That was not the case. Mother worked outside the home, helped pay the bills, and managed the household budget. Clearly, she loved my Dad, honored him, and submitted to him. We all knew who was boss.

The buck stopped with Dad—not because he bossed us around, but because he was Dad. There was never a question or an option to submit or not submit. We honored Dad by doing what he said. Not only did we do what he said, but we also cooked his favorite meals and endured endless baseball games on radio and television. We did not do these things because he forced us. We did it because we loved him.

The training I received as a young girl instilled in me a respect for authority. I naturally obeyed my teachers in school, and later in my life, I obeyed my employers and did what they said. When I fell in love with Larry, I responded to him in the same submissive way. I had little difficulty relating to Larry in the same honoring manner as I had been accustomed to with my Dad.

A MATTER OF THE HEART

Submission is not just an action of obedience, i.e.: doing what someone says. It is a heart attitude of love and respect, honoring others as more important than you. It comes naturally when you have learned to respect authority. However, if as a child you were allowed to disobey and get your own way, argue until your parents caved in, you will have to work at developing a submitted heart.

We should not fear submission. You do not lose your identity or minimize your self-value when you submit. You actually display strength. A submitted heart does not have to prove itself. You do not have to prove your point and show you are right, leaving others to be wrong.

When you choose to live with a submitted, surrendered spirit, you will argue less. If you are right, you do not have to prove it. Right eventually proves itself. If you are wrong, submission protects you. Your wrongs will not consume you. A person with a heart of submission even allows others to be wrong without heaping on them shame or blame.

I once listened to a group of women discuss this topic. I heard several of them emphasize the importance of agreement rather than submission in a marriage relationship. One woman chimed in with comments about the equality of men and women. Interestingly, I noticed their voices change tones when they even mentioned the word "submit." They spoke with tones of disgust, disapproval, and defensiveness; 'challenging' could summarize their attitudes.

These were not abused women whose husbands treated them unfairly and insensitively. These women were godly leaders—educated, independent thinkers who read their Bibles and attended prayer meetings. However, our culture had also influenced their thinking. These women, not wanting to be 'weak,' would certainly not follow their husbands' initiatives without seeking a compromise and calling it an "agreement."

Ladies, allow your husband to initiate and follow his suggestions and ideas. Listen to his point-of-view and support him in his way of thinking without always seeking to change his perspective. If his way is a different way than yours and it will lead you to the same desired destination, honor him by doing things his way. He will do the same for you.

HOW TO AGREEABLY DISAGREE

You may ask, "But what if we do not agree?" Let me clarify. A submitted heart is not always a silent voice. A submitted heart respects another person enough to confidently express an opposing opinion with self-control, articulate communication, and support for the viewpoint using a tactful approach. When you state your case, you may enter into a discussion that leads to a batting back and forth of ideas and philosophies. At this point, both husband and wife test the submitted heart.

Ask yourself:

+ "Am I out of control with my emotions?"
+ "Do I intend to prove my partner wrong?"
+ "Is it important to me to get my way?"

If you answer "yes" to these questions, you lose even if you win. However, if you do come to an impasse, God has provided a referee in His Word. He desires that we submit to one another, but ultimately, the fifth chapter of Ephesians says, *"Wives, submit to your own husbands, as to the Lord"* (Ephesians 5:22).

Yikes! What if he is wrong? I will tell you that this definitely happens. Have I ever had the right answer that Larry would not hear, therefore, I submitted to his decision and it was wrong? Yes. What was the result? We lived in harmony, not with the goal of finger pointing to prove who was right or wrong, but we aimed to live in unity. When I submitted and he was wrong, we lived together in the consequences of the wrong decision, and God honored both of us in the process. Larry learned a lesson, and I lived in unity and love with my husband.

The table turns. Larry has also submitted to me when I pressed him to see my wisdom. I remember one instance when my "wisdom" proved to be a dumb and selfishly motivated persuasion. In order to give me my way, he gave in to me and compromised his sense of good judgment. At the time, it looked like agreement when in reality, he submitted to me rather than me submitting to him. Even today, when we are at the point that we discover that we have made a wrong decision, we admit it together, do not blame each other, repent and unify. God is not so concerned with whether you are right or wrong; He looks for a humble, contrite heart—a submitted, surrendered heart to one another and to Him.

What do we fight against--submission or authority? In women's liberation, have we come to resent others telling us what to do? Do our efforts to control our own lives often cause us to control others? Some say, "My husband does not have authority over me; we share an equal partnership. I am not submitting to the authority of my husband." Yes, each of you are equally valuable, but both of you are not at the "head of the line" in your marriage. The scripture clearly states that in marriage, the husband is the "head of the wife." No government, corporation, church, or family works effectively when led by two "CEOs." All institutions have one CEO—the head, who empowers all of his co-laborers to accomplish their goal in unity.

Let's talk about authority and how it affects our lives.

AUTHORITY IS UNIVERSAL

Authority is everywhere. The authority principle goes into operation the moment we are born. The human spirit must surrender to authority or it cannot survive in peace. When we resist authority, we live dissatisfied and miserable. Submission to authority brings security and contentment to our human souls. It releases us rather than restricts us.

Resisting authority takes so much negative energy. Think of a child who chooses to disobey. It takes so much energy to resist his parent's plea to "Come here." He runs away. Then, when his parents find him, he fights, resists, throws a fit, cries, and eventually collapses in exhaustion. Submitting would have been so much easier and much more rewarding.

Since authority is a universal law, who am I to think that I can defy that law and still experience the positive outcome that this absolute principle creates? A fundamental principle has no exceptions. In the same way, what scientist would try to prove that the law of conservation of energy has exceptions? There simply are no exceptions. Why would I even want to try to disprove a universal principle? To respect authority and to bend my will to that authority, whether it is a traffic policeman, the IRS, the administration, or my husband, brings the satisfaction of peace in my life. It removes my striving, the use of negative energy, and protects me from being ruled in my heart by negative emotions—fear, anger, offense and bitterness.

> Submission to authority brings security and contentment to our human souls.

Recently, we moved into our new home and I wanted to create a new bed to plant a row of trimmed boxwood scrubs lining the pathway to our backyard. In order for these plantings to rightly align with our gate, the pathway needed to encroach my neighbor's property line by thirty-six square inches. I asked my neighbor for permission to do this.

Anytime you ask someone else for permission to do something, prepare to submit to his or her answer. I was highly motivated to enhance our yard in a very tasteful, formal garden style; yet, when I asked for permission, I stated that I would agree to their decision whether yea or nay. However, I really thought they would give only one answer--"yes." The afternoon passed and they replied that they did not want me to intrude their property line. Not even one square inch. My question to them gave them authority over me. Now, I faced the decision to submit, honor my neighbors, and not harbor resentment, or to submit, think of their insensitivity every time I saw them, and create a silent wedge in our relationship.

In life, we face multitudes of opportunities almost daily to submit and be satisfied, to submit and be resentful, or to create enemies by not submitting and doing our own thing. Choosing to submit and respect another person's authority liberates us and allows us to bear the fruitfulness of peaceful living. There is no garden design worth creating an uncomfortable relationship with my neighbors. They probably see something that I cannot see and their decision could protect me in the future. In reality, true submission always wins. A truly submitted heart stays grateful, even when the answer is "no."

In order to fully embrace this principle, it may help to picture the following images of the word 'submit' and its synonym 'yield.' When I merge onto a highway with traffic racing by at seventy miles per hour, I observe signs that say 'yield.' In my previous state of residence, the entrance signs on highway ramps said 'merge.' To 'merge' and to 'yield' hold two very different meanings.

Yield means to defer to or acquiesce, to give in to. To merge means to combine, join together, fuse. In marriage, a wife yields so our lives can merge. If we forge forward into the fast paced traffic insisting on our own rights without yielding while we merge, we will most likely shed unnecessary blood. When I yield and look for my place to merge into ongoing traffic, that traffic adjusts its speed and allows me to become one, to join together with its flow. We unify because we both adjust our pace. This is the satisfying reward of living a submitted life.

5

[HE Says]

◑

THE CURSE OF CRITICISM
By Larry

THOUGH PAUL FAILS to mention it in his first letter to the Corinthian church, I'm positive that many husbands and wives believe that one more gift should be added to the list of spiritual gifts in chapter twelve—the gift of criticism. Most often, this gift manifests itself among couples shortly after they say, "I do." It consists of delivering regular put-downs and belittling remarks. It specializes in exposing faults, harping on weaknesses, condemning constantly, and engaging in miscellaneous forms of nitpicking. In the end, the silver-tongued condemner stands as the victor and the vanquished becomes a cowering failure, lacking any sense of value or self-confidence.

The gift of criticism is quite often exercised by just one of the marriage partners, who, in the early stages of the marriage, feels that his calling in life is to change his mate. The goal is to make the necessary changes to see her transformed into his own image. It requires that the "gifted" spouse reveal, expose, and magnify every perceived fault in the seemingly less "gifted" partner. Unless other faults become exposed during the process, the ultimate intended result is the perfection of one's mate. Hallelujah!

Things heat up a bit when both partners are "talented" at criticism. This double blessing (curse) generally arrives when both partners can skillfully participate in verbal boxing matches. In this scenario, they try to outdo each other with snippets of sarcasm and tit for tat vocal jabs. Neither one is willing to back down when attacked. Each person's goal is to verbally out spar the other with hurtful words until he or she achieves a knockout punch. Sometimes, the boxing match can go on for months and even years. Unfortunately, the competition never really ends and the scars can last a lifetime.

THE DEVASTATION OF CRITICISM

Whether criticism comes mostly from one partner or both, the end result is the same—devastation. Neither spouse rises to his full potential while being attacked by the other. The "gift of criticism" is obviously the fruit of the human, carnal spirit, rather than the fruit of the Holy Spirit. What is it in human nature that is more prone to see and point out the partner's weaknesses rather than the partner's strengths? Why would a husband destroy the self-worth in his wife, or a wife discredit her husband's sense of value? Why is it easier to defame a person than to encourage a person? Either choice requires the same amount of words.

There is nothing more devastating than the unleashed, uncontrolled tongue. It can make failures out of even the most potential-filled partners. Do we really know the devastating effects of continual criticism? No one can survive it. James, a writer in the New Testament, proves a good point in the third chapter of his letter that the tongue is set on fire in hell, and carries within its sting a world of iniquity.

WHY CRITICIZE YOUR MATE?

1. The Infection of Insecurity

Insecure people tear down others—bottom line. I'm convinced that we criticize our mates in part because we're unhappy with ourselves. We don't like who we are, and our low self-esteem reveals itself in the way we treat our spouses.

When counseling young men who are considering making a marriage commitment to a young lady, I always ask one question. It may surprise you that my first question is never, "Is she born-again?" That's my second question. The first question is, "When you're with her, does she build you up or tear you down?" If the man answers, "She sometimes (or often) tears me down," then I strongly counsel him, "Run for your life! It's unlikely you will ever succeed in life or ministry with a spouse who berates you."

> I'm convinced that we criticize our mates in part because we're unhappy with ourselves.

The same question applies for a young lady. "When you're in the presence of the man of your dreams, do you feel edified or beaten down?" The answer will tell you whether to proceed or flee. It doesn't matter if he acts like the world's most spiritual man; if a young lady feels beaten down when she's around that man, she should drop everything and run! I've seen too many women destroyed by those self-proclaimed men of God. Soon after the wedding of such a man, he turns into Attila the Hun and she becomes his emotional slave.

2. The Scourge of Self-righteousness

Self-righteousness can also lead a person to criticize his or her mate. A self-righteous spouse can berate his or her partner for not being spiritual enough. Regardless of how hard the person tries, the poor victim of spiritual harassment never fully makes the grade. Even if the person expends the greatest amount of effort, his or her determination never satisfies the critical partner.

Self-righteous women will try to dominate a marriage through a variety of methods ranging from manipulation to condemnation. Through subtle (sometimes not so subtle) pressure to conform her husband to her set of religious rules, the wife continually prods him with statements like the following: "Read the Bible more;" "Pray more;" "Attend church more often;" and "Act more spiritual!" All the time that she pressures him to be the spiritual head of the house, she is, in fact, driving him further away. I'm sure these women believe that it's easier for them to make their husbands spiritual than it is to trust the Holy Spirit. Or at least they feel the Holy Spirit could surely use their help.

Legalism is often the self-righteous male's tactic. Unlike women, a critical man tends to use legalism rather than manipulation or condemnation to enforce his convictions. For him, it's the letter of the law that counts. Grace is out of the question. He may say, "I said it and that settles it. God and I are synonymous. You will be spiritual because I said so!" The more self-righteous he becomes, the more criticism is leveled at the wife and family members. No one is exempt from this highly critical spirit.

A legalistic man is always heavy-handed. He serves God out of obligation rather than out of joy or love. All of his criticisms come in the form of condemnation. And pity the wife or children who love to have fun. A legalist considers fun a form of carnality and sin. I feel sorry for the wife and children who grow up under this self-righteous spiritual domination.

3. The Poison of Perfectionism

Perfectionism is a third source of a critical attitude. The fastidious husband or wife can take punctilious, flawless, meticulous demands into whole new realms of pain. Perfectionists are masters of misery. They know how to make everyone despondent, including themselves. Their purist lifestyles always bleed onto everyone and everything within their sphere of influence.

Praise God, I'm not a perfectionist, but I was at one time. I could pick out the speck in your eye a mile away. Through the telescopic lens of my judgmental attitude, I could point out your faults without ever knowing you. I could criticize things that didn't even merit criticizing. I could find fault with your house, your kids, your hair, your lack of hair, your clothes, your dirty carpet, your mean and ugly dog, your dandruff, or your lack of deodorant. I could criticize the way you walked, talked and flossed. I could criticize your theology. I could criticize your methodology. I could criticize your cosmology. I could disapprove of your etymology. I could pass judgment on your musicology. I could condemn your eschatology. And woe to the person who didn't have an "-ology" for me to censure.

Then I got married. Oh, God help me! I soon began to discover that perfectionism is sin. No, it's SIN! The perfectionist is the ultimate of nit-pickers. He can find fault in everyone and everything. For starters, my wife didn't put the lid on the toothpaste. Worse yet, she squeezed the tube from the middle! Obviously, she had never read the directions on the side of the box— a must for a perfectionist. And what was most egregious was the night I noticed my toothbrush was wet before I used it. I nearly ruptured before the rapture! My response was, "What? Just because you forgot your toothbrush at home doesn't mean you can use mine!"

Then came the day when I discovered she put the roll of toilet paper on the spool upside down. It was a dark day indeed. Can you imagine? I ask you, CAN YOU IMAGINE? Do you realize how traumatic that can be for a perfectionist? For men that are on the go, how can you go fast when the toilet paper is upside down? Aren't you glad the day arrived when God showed me that He desires excellence, but not perfection? Yes, and so is everyone else. I've been born-again, again.

It's especially hard on a perfectionist when he encounters another one. Let me illustrate with a personal experience. I once sat in a restaurant with my arm on the top of the booth cushion. A man sitting in the booth behind me got up from his seat, came over to where I sat, and tapped me on the shoulder. "You're about to touch my Mom." "Oh, I'm sorry," I responded, noticing for the first time his aged mother sitting behind me. "Did I touch your Mom?" "No," he replied, "but you're about to!"

I had just come in contact with a member of that lovely race of people who cannot tolerate imperfection in the imperfect people around them. His standard seems high because he finds all human foibles, weaknesses, mistakes, sins, and failures to be inexcusable. No, his standard isn't Jesus or the Bible, but himself. If you don't measure up to his perfectionist requirements, he slates you for his critical list. And once you get on his "list," it's hard to get off. Why? Because you'll probably keep committing the same unpardonable mistakes that put you there in the first place. Hell for the perfectionist is to discover that he is not perfect.

The bottom line, short and simple, is that perfectionism is a sin that requires repentance. No one is perfect, including the perfectionist. If your ultimate goal in life is to work as a spiritual surgeon so you can remove the speck out of everyone else's eyes—especially the eyes of your spouse—first take the log out of your own. Otherwise, you lack the qualifications to perform the surgery.

4. The Sin of Self-promotion

Self-promotion is another source of criticism. In my opinion, men are more culpable in this area. This is the insecure man who deludes himself into thinking that the only way he can build himself up is to belittle his wife. And most of the time, he does it on a subconscious level, not even knowing his motivation. But other people see the results. The poor wife has to endure repeated humiliation and put-downs in front of others so that his macho image can be stroked. But he must realize that when he publicly degrades his wife, he destroys himself as well. You cannot simultaneously build yourself up while tearing your wife down. In Ephesians 5:28, Paul considers wife hatred the same as self-hatred because she and the husband are one. What the husband does to his wife, he does to himself. Husbands, if you demean your wife, you ultimately devastate yourself. It's that simple.

5. Selfishness: The Ultimate Destroyer

For whatever reason a spouse would belittle the other, it always boils down to one word—"self." Selfishness is the major destroyer of marriage and leadership. Criticism in marriage would quickly die for lack of use if it weren't for selfishness raising its ugly head in the relationship.

PATTERNS CAN BE BROKEN

The good news is that we can exchange criticism for edification and encouragement. How can a person who is critical by nature change his or her personality to that of an encourager? God, after all, is a *lifter of my head* (Psalm 3:3). Numerous solutions exist to help a partner grow into his or her full potential. Who better to help deliver us from destructive habit patterns than a loving, sensitive spouse?

We can exchange criticism for edification and encouragement.

How can we break destructive patterns of verbal abuse? What are the antidotes? There are several.

1. *Remove Your Own Log*

Jesus makes it clear in Matthew 7:3-5 that if I wish to remove a speck from another's eye, I must first remove the log in my own eye. And it really works. When I find myself criticizing something my wife is doing, I stop and say to myself, "Larry, you're being critical about something that Devi is doing. At the same time, you are totally ignoring your own negative habits. If you'll change your own negative habits first, then you can address her issues." The funny thing is that as soon as I start removing the log in my own eye, I soon forget why she irritated me in the first place.

2. *Turn the Negative Into a Positive*

Turn the negative irritation into a positive attribute. You can always find something positive in what you previously considered negative. Look for it. It's there. Remember that God does not call you to change the other person. That's the job of the Holy Spirit. He only calls you to change yourself. That passage is recorded in Titus 1:1; <u>Larry</u> Titus 1:1, that is.

3. *Choose to Love*

Love is a choice. It is a decision, not an emotion. Paul writes in I Corinthians 13 the following truths:

+ Love remembers no wrongs
+ Love does not keep record of past hurts
+ Love does not envy other's successes
+ Love chooses to believe the best in a person

Peter expresses a similar thought when he pens these words, ". . . *love covers a multitude of sins*" (I Peter 4:8).

4. *Be Patient*

God is patient with you. Extend to your partner the same grace that God gives you.

5. *Speak Edifying Words*

Speak only words that build up the other person. In Ephesians 4:29, Paul challenges us to stop any unwholesome, cancerous words before they come out of our mouths. We must choose only words that edify and encourage. Remember, we are not part of the destruction crew, but the construction crew. If our words do not build up, we should not use them. Sometimes, we speak our most hateful words to those we love the most. God help us!

6. *Don't Speak Immediately*

When something bothers you and you believe that the issue needs to be addressed, wait. Let your emotions die down until you can see the other person's perspective. Don't give your spouse a piece of your mind, if it denigrates. Also, wisely remember that anytime you give a person a piece of your mind, it always leaves less for you.

A SUPPORTIVE SPOUSE

I love to use my wife as an example of one who knows how to effectively use diplomacy and sensitivity when bringing to my attention things that need changing. I never feel that she is in the attack mode, but instead she shows genuine interest in my welfare. And of course, I, like many men, am defensive by nature, so it's important that we have spouses who know when and how to bring areas of concern to our attention.

I do not know of many successful leaders whose spouses continually tear them down. In fact, I can't think of any. On the other hand, I can name hundreds of excellent leaders whose wives or husbands support and encourage them. If you do not publicly and privately build up your mate, it matters little who else does. To have your wife or husband as the President of your Fan Club is the ultimate of blessings.

TWO WORDS MUST GO

Ban two words from your vocabulary--the oxymoronic words "constructive criticism." They contradict each other. Construction builds something beautiful. Criticism is barbed, hurtful, insensitive, and selfishly motivated. It always destroys. It is not motivated by love, but by a judgmental attitude on the part of the offender. So, criticism can never be constructive. A mature person wants to be corrected when he's wrong—even if he's as defensive as I am. But no one can continually endure criticism without it destroying his sense of value and self-worth.

THE PARABLE OF A ROSE

Sammy Jo Barbour, an inmate at the Iowa State Penitentiary, mailed me a parable that he had written after seeing Devi and me on Celebration, a television program hosted by Joni and Marcus Lamb from the Daystar Network in Dallas, Texas:

> A certain man planted a rose and watered it faithfully. Before it blossomed, he examined it and saw the bud that would soon blossom, but noticed thorns upon the stem and thought, "How can any beautiful flower come from a plant burdened with so many sharp thorns?"

> Saddened by his thought, he neglected to water the rose and before it was ready to bloom, it died.

> So it is with many people. Within every soul there is a rose. We have God-like qualities planted in us at birth growing amid the thorns of our faults. Many of us look at ourselves and see only the thorns, the defects. We despise ourselves, thinking that nothing good can possibly come from us. We neglect to water the good within us and eventually, it dies. We never realize our potential.

Some people do not see the rose within themselves. Someone else might show it to them. One of the greatest gifts a person can possess is the ability to reach past the thorns and find the rose within others. This characterizes love—to look at people and know their true faults, yet accept them into your life and recognize the nobility in their souls. Help them to realize that they can overcome their faults. If we show them the rose, they will conquer their thorns. Only then will they blossom many times over.

Within every soul, there is a rose.

This parable made me supremely grateful for Devi. Praise God for my leader/wife who has spent her life choosing to ignore my thorns and cultivate my roses!

THE CURSE OF CRITICISM
By: Devi

L ARRY AMAZES ME. Obviously, he uses irony to captivate your attention and communicate a poignant truth—a truth that is essential for you to embrace, especially when leaders live together. The truth is that criticism in all forms is a curse, not a gift! It remains impossible to reach one's goals in life while regularly living under the dark cloud of disapproval. Criticism creates self-doubt. And no one continues to achieve when self-doubt prevails.

LEADERS ARE TARGETS

I wanted my husband to succeed. He worked in full time ministry when we married, and I felt honored to be a pastor's wife. I must admit that I fantasized about the life of a minister's family. I saw his profession up there along with the mayor of the city, the doctors, and the lawyers. I grew up in a family who respected clergy and so did I have high regard for those who served in ministry. Not long after we accepted our first pastorate, however, I learned differently. Somehow, the important person that I married was not necessarily seen as important by everyone. In fact, I quickly realized that he was a target for criticism. Not only did people criticize Larry, but me and our children as well.

> Criticism creates self-doubt.

I soon learned that the best defense against others' attempts to destroy my husband's success was to do all I could to edify him. While others tore him down, I built him up. I was the one who had the most influence to drive self-doubt out of his life.

It's not that I did not see his faults; it's just that his virtues appeared so much greater. I clearly saw my assigned role in this battle against criticism. Why would I choose to sit idly by and watch him struggle under the attacks of critical people? After all, if he succeeded, I would also receive the blessings. If he failed, I would suffer. Why then would I choose to create or enforce self-doubt by pointing out his faults?

THE POWER OF WORDS

Words have power! They have the power to build up or they have the power to tear down. My favorite scripture—a guide for my life—is in Ephesians.

> *Let no corrupting talk come out of your mouths, but only such as is good for building up, as fits the occasion, that it may give grace to those who hear.* Ephesians 4:29

I believe it is in everyone's carnal nature to find fault in others. This is a low level of living. However, when we truly walk in the Spirit, we choose to overcome carnal ways and apply the truth to our lives. The more secure you become in Christ, the easier it is to build others up.

It is so embarrassing and uncomfortable in social situations when other couples punch and jab one another with words. The atmosphere becomes stifling—as if you can't breathe. Certainly, you know not to laugh, and you really want to cry. How sad it is to puncture love with such cruel and unkind words.

WORDS CAN RECOIL

The destructive wife is one who constantly tears down her husband. She nags, belittles, and berates. She even does so in the presence of their children. How unwise! She doesn't realize the long term effects of her critical ways. The initial consequences of disparaging her husband in front of their children will cause them to develop a lack of respect for their father. However, as they get older, they will see things more clearly, end up disrespecting her, and disrespecting themselves as well.

A young woman told me her story. She explained that she grew up in a single parent home, raised by her mother after her parents divorced. She related that her mother had painted a picture of her father as being an awful, demon-like man. As a girl, she was deprived of having a relationship with her father because of bitterness between her parents. Only later, after becoming an adult, did she reunite with her Dad. She found him to be a practical, hard working, and caring person. As a child, she had viewed her mother as a victim.

Now, having a clearer perspective, she questions her mother's truthfulness regarding her father's character. She now understands her mother's critical, self-righteous, and manipulative nature. She lovingly maintains a relationship with both parents, but clearly sees the devastating results of her mother's condemnation towards her father.

Criticism never reaps good consequences. What you hope to achieve will always turn on you. Everyone loses.

THE BLIND SIDE

For ten consecutive years, I met with a small group of ladies who were significant influencers. Each year, we spent five days together talking, praying, and eating, with no particular agenda. We named ourselves "SWAT" sisters. SWAT was a self-made acronym for Submitted Women And Thankful. We were diverse in many ways, but what we shared in common was our love for God's Word and our love for our husbands. For me, this was a personal time of evaluation before the Lord in preparation for the coming year. I distinctly remember asking God, "What do you want me to improve in my life this year?" One year, He told me to talk less and listen more. I did this; it is now a habit. But much to my surprise, the Holy Spirit hit me on my blind side. This year, this is what I heard in my spirit. "Devi, you are critical and judgmental." YIKES! I argued with God. How can this be? I rehearsed in my mind previous conversations. I rehearsed times of negotiations, disapprovals, and conflicts. I always wanted the best for others. I didn't berate or belittle my husband. I just could not accept this to be true. I didn't see it. God's gentle and loving voice said to me, "You don't see it because you call it 'discernment'".

To discern means to perceive or to recognize something. My mind thinks quickly. I come to conclusions and make decisions without delay. I am naturally talkative and I am naturally a teacher. I like to tell others what I know, whether it is about a book that I am reading or a recipe that is worth cooking. Add that all together, and guess what you get: a lesson, a correction, instruction, a direction, a suggestion. Because my heart is not ill willed, I never would have thought that this all could add up to making a judgment about others that I should not make or criticizing someone else for not aligning to my standards.

I get it! God knew my vulnerabilities; my strengths were vulnerable to become my weakness. He nailed me. He knew that I looked at people from the perspective of how I could improve them rather than how I could support them. The difference is a top-down approach rather than a humble bottom up approach. My adult daughter had tried to tell me this for years, but I just could not see it. I listened to her and tried to understand her loving words of correction, but didn't see it until God got hold of me.

For one year, I took notice. (And still do.) First, I listened to my thoughts. When I entered a hotel lobby and wanted to adjust the art, lower its level and make it straight, I stopped, changed my way of thinking and looked at the painting. I appreciated the colors and design rather than wanting to re-hang the picture. Then, I took notice of when I wanted to give others instructions, keeping them from learning on their own by making mistakes. It is a fine line to walk, discerning, but not judging or criticizing.

Jesus' famous line, quoted by even those who do not believe, is, "*Judge not, that you be not judged.*" This is verse 1 of Matthew chapter 7. He goes on to explain that it is common to try to remove a speck in someone else's eye when we have a log in our own. I understood this and honestly, constantly worked to whittle away my own logs. Maybe this is why I still lived with my blind side. In Matthew 7:6, Jesus said, "*...do not throw your pearls before pigs, lest they trample them underfoot and turn to attack you.*" My question was, "How do you know who the pigs are unless you judge another to be a pig?" Good question.

Here is what I learned. Having good judgment and being judgmental are two very different things. Having good judgment is the ability to make a considered decision. Judgmental is having an excessively critical point of view, according to the dictionary definition. With this understanding, over the course of one year, I was able to convert my critical, judgmental attitude to one that makes well considered decisions—especially the decision to speak to others from a bottom-up position, encouraging them rather than instructing or correcting them.

Larry is the benefactor of my improvement and so is my family. If I can change, so can you. Thank you, Holy Spirit, for being my Helper. Not only am I grateful, but others are also.

6

[HE Says]

ME MACHO

By: Larry

Y OU CAN NEARLY hear the grunts of Tarzan as he swings from tree limb to tree limb. Finally, he hits the ground with a thud and bellows out his famous yell. "Ah-ee-ah-ee-ah-ee." Then he turns to Jane, pounding his chest, yelling, "Me macho, me the leader." Then, of course, Jane, having read Ephesians 5:21, willingly submits to her spiritual stud with a dismissive, "Of course, you are, honey. And I humbly submit to your spiritual authority."

DON'T BE AN APE-MAN!

In unhealthy marriages, Tarzan usually gets to rule the relationship. You can identify him by his dented chest, having been made concave by his macho ravings and chest beatings. This kind of man knows strong, unilateral leadership, but doesn't know the give and take of normal leadership. He only knows the take side. He maintains authority by fear tactics, fits of anger, financial control, intimidation, secrecy, moodiness, selfishness, and suppression of his wife and children. He exerts absolute dominance over the home environment. He often feels free to extend emotional and/or physical abuse, and occasionally, makes a great decision that causes him to look better than he really is.

It is critical for strong male leaders to share leadership with the rest of the family members and, in particular, with their spouses. This not only creates a healthy balance in the home, which produces healthy family members, but it gives the man the ability and freedom to become all God intends. Unfortunately, domineering male leaders keep their followers anemic and weak.

In a healthy marriage, the pendulum of leadership swings back and forth between the husband and wife. A healthy balance of leadership between the spouses needs to exist. Both husband and wife know their respective areas of ability and expertise and yield to the other when a task or decision is more suited to their partner's abilities.

Don't Be a Wimp Either!

The opposite of the dominant male leader is equally weak. He fits the description of a sheepish, wimpish, nondescript, milquetoast, abdicating, cringing, effete, and indecisive man. He most often quotes the response, "Yes, dear." This man doesn't swing from trees or bushes. Swinging from trees proves to be too dangerous, and romping through bushes can create a rash. He might consent to pruning them, if he has gloves to wear, so the pruning shears don't chaff his hands. You know how much lotions cost these days. Virtually, all of these good, but timid, men possess a tremendous fear of their wives. This fear immobilizes them from making effective decisions, and, in turn, prevents them from winning the respect that they long for from their wives. In fact, because they fear making the wrong decision, they will most likely not make any decisions.

I heard an example of this type of man several years ago, told in typical apocryphal form by a preacher wanting to exaggerate a point. It was said that St. Peter, in an attempt to screen the newly arrived candidates for heaven, instructed all the men who had not been henpecked by their wives to stand in one particular reserved section in the celestial city. From that area, they would be assigned their mansion. With one exception, they all obediently complied by moving into their holding room. But one little timid man cowered in the corner. "Why aren't you standing with the rest of the men?" the revered Apostle demanded. "Because my wife told me to stand over here." Ha! Ha! Tee Hee! It's cute if you haven't heard it before, but it speaks a truth that appears to fit too many men in today's generation. Most were raised by mothers, grandmothers, or aunts, and grew up without having a strong pant leg to hold on to. They had no male role models to mentor them.

I find the crestfallen, defeated men that fit this description more sad than pathetic. We are rearing a generation of passive men that desperately need role models. We need strong, spiritual, balanced, and sensitive male leaders who will take these men under their coat tails and help them escape the paralysis and pain of this lifestyle.

While the Bible gives several examples of weak, timid, and diffident leaders, they don't seem to be the type of men that God is drawn to. The reason is because retiring and shy men rarely demonstrate the authority that is needed to represent God. In the same way, however, the Lord rarely calls upon the Tarzan types either. One refuses to use authority, while the other only knows how to abuse it. Both extremes can disqualify one from God's use.

BE A MAN'S MAN

Elijah, the man who became John the Baptist's model and the one in Malachi 4:5 that the prophet commands us to emulate, was a "Man's Man!" He came onto the scene with a zeal for the Lord that both decimated Jezebel's prophets and defied Ahab's blasphemies. His word had the power to stop the heavens from raining for three and a half years and the compassion to feed a widow and her son, enabling them to live through a famine. Resident in Elijah was a personality that could be as tough as nails when dealing with tyrants and as soft as velvet when caring for a despairing mother.

Don't feel that you have to make a choice between the extreme of all bluster and bravado and the opposite extreme of soft, retiring and aloof. God wants you balanced. He's looking for leaders who exercise authority, but who also show kindness. He wants men to be powerful, yet compassionate. Your sword needs to be sharp on one side and gentle on the other.

When John the Baptist arrived on the scene hundreds of years later, Jesus said that He had come in the spirit of Elijah. To prove His point, Jesus asked the crowd a very probing question:

> "What did you go out into the wilderness to see? A reed shaken by the wind? What then did you go out to see? A man dressed in soft clothing? Behold, those who are dressed in splendid clothing and live in luxury are in kings' courts. What then did you go out to see? A prophet? Yes, I tell you, and more than a prophet." Luke 7:24-26

Jesus actually asked the populace if they came out of their towns and villages to witness an effeminate preacher. Obviously, His rhetorical question did not need a reply. When God asks a question, He does not want a reply, only a response.

Jesus wanted the crowds to take notice that John the Baptist did not exemplify effeminacy or softness. So, what was His point? Simple! God won't send out a herald who doesn't properly represent Him. Men are not attracted to timid, pathetic, mealy-mouthed men. Neither are women and neither is God.

A woman may be initially attracted to the sensitivity of a timid man before they marry. However, if she discovers, after marriage, that his sensitivity is a cover-up for an indecisive, sheepish nature, she will immediately lose respect for him. So will everyone else.

Who would you go out into the wilderness to see? There is not much that would draw me to the wilderness to see anyone. I might go to a national forest, to the Pacific Ocean, or to a Caribbean Island to see someone. If I did go to the wilderness to hear or see someone, I would want to encounter John the Baptist, Jesus, Elijah, or someone else that exudes authority. The person I would go to the wilderness to see would also need to command respect, demand repentance, and know when it's the right time to back off and yield authority to one who has authority over him. Otherwise, I wouldn't be available.

I believe that when Jesus comes again, His selection process will probably resemble how it was when He came the first time. He will choose men who properly reflect His character.

A MAN'S MAN FOR ALL TIME

When Jesus came onto the scene, His natural authority distinguished Him from the teachers of the law and endeared Him to the crowds. After all, He came to a people who had endured centuries of tyrannical rule. This Man's contrasting leadership style of leading by example rather than force became immediately recognized and appreciated. The Leader of all leaders knew how to be humble, quiet, sensitive, compassionate, and peaceable. Only twice did His zeal become overtly intense, and that was for the purpose of cleansing His Father's house. What a man. What a man's man. What a perfect role model for the rest of us.

I resent the paintings from the Middle Ages that have made Jesus look effeminate and beautiful. The artists who created these paintings hired models to pose as Jesus. Of course, since none of these artists actually saw Jesus, they had to hire stand-ins that fit their idea of what Jesus looked like. Obviously, they had never read Isaiah's description of Christ as indescribably homely (Isaiah 53), or that of John the Beloved's as One with flaming eyes and a voice that sounded like rushing waters (Revelation 1). No effeminacy here.

Unfortunately, these caricatures from the Middle Ages paintings have stuck. For hundreds of years, we have had images of Jesus in every home and bookstore that make him look more like a salesman at a department store cosmetic counter than a carpenter with rough and splintered hands. I just can't imagine Jesus offering me a limp-wristed handshake when He returns in glory. Can you? Not from the One who will rule the nations of the world with an iron rod. By the way, if someone suggests that you should get in touch with your feminine side, tell him or her that the only feminine side you have is your wife, and that you're in touch with her every day—literally.

It's hard for mild mannered, gentle, laid-back men to relate to Jesus' zeal in cleansing the temple. Likewise, they may find it difficult to identify with John the Baptist ranting at the river with grasshoppers clogging his esophagus or with Elijah calling down fire from heaven on the prophets of Baal before sending them to an early grave. Now, we do have a lot of men more than happy to engage in those exploits—with or without the Spirit's leading. But for the man with a meek disposition, it is just not natural for him to use force. I relate. I'm such a man. I prefer staying distant. I'm somewhat reclusive, uncomfortable with anything that demands confrontation. I'm nervous as all get out when it comes to assuming authority. How are we, who are gentler in nature, supposed to lead in this foreign and uncomfortable environment?

WHETHER YOU FEEL LIKE IT OR NOT

In the Introduction to this book, I describe how I lead by conviction and obligation. Both of these motivations come from the Word of God. I have a deep conviction that God calls all men to be heads, and therefore, we must lead. I also know, biblically, that God has delegated me and all men to extend His authority; therefore, I am obligated to exercise authority whenever it is needed. It is my job to do so. I can't say that I have ever enjoyed being authoritative, but it's a responsibility that I accept for the sake of maintaining unity, peace and harmony in my marriage and family.

How I exercise authority is another story. I've tried, at times, to use authority in a highhanded, overbearing way, but it isn't me. The approach that I feel most comfortable with and that fits my personality best is to deliver the mandate with little volume and with emotions under control. I want as much as possible to understand the heart of the person or persons that are being affected.

Try picturing Joshua standing on a hill top in Ephraim, screaming at the top of his lungs with veins protruding from his neck. Imagine him saying, "Listen to me, you bunch of rebellious, rapscallion, rogue Jews. I'm sick and tired of you vacillating between gods. I've decided what I'm going to do, and if you don't want to go to Sheol, you'd better do it anyway. As for me and my house, we're going to serve the Lord. Did you hear that, kids? Well, if you'd shut up and stop playing around with your slingshots, you would have heard me. Now go back to the tent and eat your bagels." I just can't imagine him saying it that way. How about you?

Instead, I think Joshua uttered his last words with pure conviction. They didn't require a lot of volume because Joshua had already made up his mind that there was only one course of action for him and his family. He would make sure that they followed it. There were no options, and no one could change his mind. Leading by pure conviction and demonstrating by example greatly inspires others to follow you.

SET THE EXAMPLE

My favorite way to dispense authority is by example. I must willingly submit to those whom God places in authority over me, if I am to expect others to obey my authority. I can't make demands from my wife and children, yet refuse to walk obediently before those in authority over me. For me to do so would be hypocrisy and it would also promote rebellion in them.

There are times when the temple of your home must be put back in order by the cleansing action of discipline and authority. At those times, Jesus won't come down in the flesh to do it for you. You can do this yourself. You must take upon yourself that part of Jesus' nature that is compassionate and, at the same time, confrontational. The steel willed conviction inside you must remain as strong and determined as that of Joshua saying, *"As for me and my house, we will serve the Lord"* (Joshua 24:15). No ifs, ands, or buts about it. And, by the way, abdication to your wife's leadership at times like this is out of the question.

God does not call men to be demanding, dictatorial, chest-thumping Jane-suppressors. He calls us men to act with decisiveness and conviction. He wants us to be character-charged Kingdom chasers. Jesus' glowing compliment of John the Baptist—the one whom He calls *"the greatest born of women"*—is His statement that John *"took the Kingdom by force"* (Matthew 11:11-15). In the same verses, He then identifies John with the spirit of Elijah. You don't need to wear garments of scratchy camel hair, eat grasshoppers, and live in the desert to fulfill God's purpose as an Elijah man. But you do have to live as a man of conviction. You do have to refuse to bow to this generation's views of either a hairy chested machismo type on steroids or to androgynous, women- wanna-bees seeking breast implants. This emasculated generation needs to have the meaning of true manhood redefined. This new definition must come from the Bible and from men who model the biblical example.

We, who live in the final days of Gentile occupation before Christ's return, must learn to move in that same spirit of Elijah. We have a biblical mandate in Malachi 4:5-6 to come in the spirit of Elijah to restore godly leadership in the homes. We have a mandate from the King of kings in Matthew 11 to forcefully advance the Kingdom of God in that same spirit of Elijah. We must make up a new generation of Elijah men:

+ Men committed to putting their families before their jobs and church.
+ Men faithful to their wives and examples to their children.
+ Role models for godliness to the young men of the world.
+ Most of all, men of courage, not afraid to stand against the kingdom of darkness.

We cannot accomplish these things through bombastic dictatorial dictums, but rather, with a spirit of humility and brokenness.

Matthew describes Jesus as one who never quarreled or argued and never raised the volume of His voice in the streets. Jesus was so gentle that He would not extinguish a smoldering wick or break a bruised reed (Matthew 12:18-21). This is what I call a "man's Man." This is the kind of leader that others will automatically follow and that the nations will put their trust in. Jesus obviously lived not out of insecurity or a need to prove Himself, but rather, He lived confidently as the person God called Him to be.

Men, regardless of your leadership style or the bend of your personality, it is still imperative that you lead. Don't abdicate your leadership responsibilities to your wives or anyone else. This is what it means to forcefully advance the Kingdom of God. After all, when Christ returns to establish His Kingdom on this earth, we want to be part of His leadership team. So, it's time to start practicing for prime time.

6

[SHE Says]

ME MACHO-ETTE
By: Devi

U NFORTUNATELY, NUMEROUS WOMEN in leadership positions possess an attitude that promotes competition with men. In order to finally seize a fair share of power in the male-dominated business world or church world and gain personal notoriety and respect, many women have felt it necessary to speak in borrowed voices—voices of men. They have convinced themselves that, in order to be heard, they should dress in business suits, sacrifice nurture and sensitivity, assert themselves, and speak tough.

In truth, this kind of action dilutes the impact of female leadership rather than strengthening it. The lie of early feminism leads us to think that there is one way—a guy's way. The lie continues with the idea that for women to lead, they must lead with the male macho style.

EMPOWERING IS SUPERIOR

Generations have passed since the initial push for equal rights. Now, after decades of sacrificing our femininity, the time has come for women to reemphasize our human birthrights to cooperation, sensitivity, and empowering of others. We naturally excel in these areas.

Both women and men stand to gain if businesses, churches and families adopt a *tender* or *gentle* strategy. A book written on this subject, *Tender Power* by Sherry Suib Cohen, clearly demonstrates through personal stories and supports by research findings the impact that gentle leadership can have on one's professional and private worlds.

The true female influence changes domineering masculine management styles to a more family environment of co-operation or team building. We call this the new model of leadership. Authors are writing books about it and corporations are benefiting from using it. But is it really new? Not for women. We are simply returning to what has always been natural and comfortable.

Leadership is about empowering others: your husband, your children, your friends, your colleagues, and your associates. When the people around you live empowered, so do you. Women have been empowering others since the time of Eve. It is an ancient female practice.

Trying to do and to be everything becomes a heavy load. In the scriptures, Jesus says it this way,

> *"Come to me, all who labour and are heavy laden, and I will give you rest. Take my yoke upon you, and learn from me, for I am GENTLE and lowly in heart, and you will find rest for your souls."* Matthew 11:28-29, (Emphasis added)

Returning to GENTLE or TENDER will lift the load that you often carry. There is power in just being nice! So, what is POWER and what is TENDER?

Plain old power, the kind that is usually practiced in a competitive environment—often a male dominated environment—typically has these characteristics:

+ It is directive.
+ It is self-protective.
+ It is not connecting to others.
+ It values the outcome over caring about people.
+ It is about facts, not feelings.
+ It is competitive.

Some descriptive words for power include: vigor, potency, pressure, energy, strength, and ability to influence. In contrast, some descriptive words for tender include: vulnerable, soft, empathic, sensitive, loving, gentle, considerate, merciful, passionate, generous, and kind.

Although the descriptive words for POWER seem to contrast those given for TENDER, look how empowering they become when we yoke them together:

+ Sensitive strength
+ Empathic leadership
+ Loving force
+ Considerate ability to influence
+ Gentle pressure

GENTLE STRENGTH

The combination of tenderness and power—I'll call it GENTLE STRENGTH—can be revolutionary. Both men and women can adopt it if they do not fear trying something new.

In Larry's discussion, he cleverly incorporates the characters Tarzan and Jane. Well, I see that Tarzan and Jane need each other. Gentle strength swinging together in unity puts *heart* in what you do—heart in your business, in your ministry, in your family, and in your marriage. Gentle strength is about partnerships. The war on sexes, viciously or subtly competing with one another, is not ordained. Instead of the "Me Tarzan, you Jane" model, husbands and wives in leadership can hold the rope together. Sometimes that means cooking together, cleaning together, stuffing envelopes together, and sharing courteously, supporting one another in whatever is needed to succeed.

Gentle strength is about empowering others—a generosity of spirit that passes knowledge on to those on the lower rungs of your ladder. Gentle strength is about empathy—the human ability to put one's self in another's shoes.

Larry is such an example of gentle strength in my life. He encourages me and corrects me—two qualities of an effective leader. When he corrects me, he uses sensitivity and empathy. If I feel embarrassed, he loves me and nurtures me until I have regained my courage. When I approach him with a "righteous appeal," pleading for him to change his mind, I enter his male ego with generous amounts of praise. Knowing that he has a tendency to get defensive, I state my concern, correction, or conviction and do not demand a decision. I submit my appeal and surrender the outcome. I give him time to respond.

When we empower one another with tenderness, we grow in personal esteem and security. It feels good to be kind. I feel better about myself when I relate to others with gentle strength. When we approach issues with coercion or aggression, everyone loses. When I approach Larry in this way, I feel unfulfilled and guilty, and he feels insecure and angry.

Men and women, husbands and wives, do not be afraid to use gentleness. Strength combined with gentleness accentuates your power. It doesn't diminish it.

7

[HE Says]

⊙⊙

LIVING WITH A LEADER
By: Larry

N THE INTRODUCTION of this book, I describe how my wife came out of the womb as a leader. Leading is as natural for her as breathing. She leads me, herself, her staff, people on a plane, anyone standing in line at a grocery checkout, the traffic, the police, the yard men, the construction crew, and, most of all, tens of thousands of women across the nation. And, I'm proud as punch of her. The greater her release and exposure, the happier I am.

I believe that God has also gifted and graced me with a few leadership skills, but nothing compared to those of my wife. I would feel totally intimidated if it weren't for two facts: Devi never displays a one-upmanship or superior attitude toward me, and she always supports my vision. I know that a secure leader would probably not need those qualities coming from his other half, but I need them.

BE BLESSED TO SEE HER BLESSED

Two major factors help me respond accordingly to Devi's leadership and keep me from becoming negative or resentful:

1. Since I'm comfortable in who God made me to be, I'm not intimated. I love what God has called me to do. I'm happy as a clam to preach, teach, disciple men, and invest in global ministries and leaders. I get tired even thinking of doing what Devi does. She moves at a killer pace and I move at a snail's pace. She wants to have fun, fun, fun, while I can hardly wait to slip away and take a nap. She wants to sit on the front pew, even when visiting a strange church, and I want to sit under the pew. She loves the limelight, and I prefer lime-lite. Most of the time, she needs a tranquilizer and I need a shot of adrenaline.

2. I enjoy seeing her excel. I don't get envious or jealous when people ask her to speak at larger conferences than the ones where I speak. I'm proud to see her moving in her gifts.

Years ago, I had a pastor call me to see if Devi and I could come and speak at his church. When I responded that I was available, but Devi wasn't, he replied, "That's okay; she was the one I really wanted." Thanks a lot, buddy. No Christmas card for you this year! Just kidding (sort of).

The truth is that I'm blessed to see her blessed. I take tremendous pride in her accomplishments. She fascinates me like she does others. I don't mind seeing her get all the attention. In fact, I'd rather the accolades go to her rather than to me.

You've heard many men introduce their wives using the hackneyed phrase, "I'd like you to meet my better half." I introduce Devi by saying, "I'd like you to meet my better three-quarters." Isn't that cute? I thought of it all by myself. No, the reason I say that is because I really believe it. She really does pull three-fourths of the leadership weight. That's not being condescending; it's being accurate. Devi can lead circles around me. And I enjoy the whirl of her activity. Like the tail of the comet, she pulls me into the gravitational force of her vision, so we can enjoy the ride together. Without her, I'd be spinning off into space.

How many men live with a woman whose leadership skills out perform their own, yet, they never experience the joy of seeing their wives blessed? I would suspect a lot. Probably a greater percentage than we could imagine.

MY MODELS OF LEADERSHIP

I think my attitude toward my wife—my lack of resentment for her leadership skills and my desire to promote her and see her blessed—came from my parents. My mother, Rachel Titus, definitely helped to mold my attitudes toward my gifts and my calling. My contentment with my own gifts and the joy and satisfaction that I have in my calling certainly came from observing her. An incredibly gifted speaker and teacher, my mother loved what she did. She kept her suitcase packed at all times and could hardly wait to board the plane for her next appointment. Like my mother, I love what I do. Now that we have grown children and I no longer carry the pastoral responsibilities of a local congregation, my pace quickens and my spirit brightens at the thought of boarding another plane and preaching to a new congregation. Why would I begrudge my wife's success when I'm so happy with mine?

My Dad has positively affected my ability to rejoice at Devi's achievements. Dad was a promoter of people and it started in his own home. To Dad, my Mom was the greatest preacher on earth. But in addition to Mom, he also promoted me. I caught him in the mall one day, bragging to a total stranger, "You should hear my son. He's just as good as Billy Graham." While I enjoyed the compliment, I was under no illusion. To compare me with Billy Graham stretched the imagination to gargantuan proportions, but that didn't matter to Dad. In Dad's eyes, I was right up there in the rarified air with the greatest evangelist on earth. I cannot remember Dad even insinuating that he resented Mom's or anyone else's success.

Dad treated my Mother with both deference and reverence. He knew how to decrease so she could increase, to step down so she could step up. In fact, he did this literally when he would introduce her to speak. Though my Dad couldn't preach a lick in the road, he would always introduce Mom before she spoke. You would think that one greater than Margaret Thatcher was about to take the podium. Mom would then walk regally to the pulpit, take the microphone, and reciprocate by honoring Dad in the same way he had honored her.

Dad firmly believed in chivalry. He was honor bound to open the door for Mom any time she approached. In fact, she wrote a poem that we read at his funeral in 1972.

WAIT FOR ME AT THE DOOR

Parting enriches the golden hours
Of memories I hold in store;
The many times you gently spoke,
"Wait, I'll open the door."

Chivalry was asserted in declining years,
As it was in days of yore;
"You be a lady and wait for me,
I'm your man and I'll get the door."

Hurriedly your hand was laid on the door
And swinging the portals wide,
You gently ushered me safely through,
Then fell in step by my side.

I'll miss your love and comfort
And your words of encouragement more;
But the thing that I'll miss the most,
You're not here to open the door.

I must learn to open my own doors
And walk on bravely through
To meet whatever lies beyond
Without the nearness of you.

For heavens realm has beckoned
And you have gone before,
But when I arrive, you'll surely say,
"Wait, I'll open the door."

Don't send Saint Peter to open the door,
Nor one of the Angels fair,
I'll expect you to greet me and welcome me in
When I make my entrance there.

—RACHEL TITUS

BETTER DISCIPLES IS AN HONOR

I cannot understand leaders who get jealous, envious, and restricting when their disciples become better than they are. That should be the greatest of compliments—when the one you have invested in excels beyond you. I love to see my wife and kids go further than I have ever gone. It brings honor to me when I can rejoice in their accomplishments.

Jesus' final prayer in John 17 was that His disciples experience the glory that the Father had given Him. The glory that the Father had shared with the Son from eternity past was now being passed down to His disciples. A great leader gladly shares his victories with those coming behind him. An insecure leader fears his spotlight will have to include others, and he does not permit that to happen.

True leaders are not only content with the success of others, but they actually delight to promote others and see them promoted. In my opinion, it takes a great man to promote and release his wife and family. Let's reverse the phrase, "Behind every great man is a woman," and say, "Behind every great woman is a man who believes in her, supports her, and isn't resentful of the fact that she's a great leader." It's a mouthful to say, but it accurately describes the attitude that men should have when married to a woman leader.

Instead of your being the "bull in the china shop," willingly let your wife be the "china in the bull shop."

7

[SHE Says]

◐

LIVING WITH A LEADER

By: Devi

HEN YOU READ Larry's words about me, he gives himself no credit. But why would he? His humility perfectly explains his leadership. When we married, Larry was in full-time ministry. His first ministry assignment out of Bible College was working with his older brother on a Native American reservation in Colorado. From there, he was music minister, preparing choral groups for pageantry and exalted praise. He traveled with his evangelist parents for a season, leading worship and preaching occasionally. Then, God gave him his assignment of leadership.

Larry took a position with a denomination of leading their statewide youth programs. His title was Northwest District Youth President. He was in this position when we married. Later, he was a men's dean in a Bible College, and after that, he fulfilled an assistant pastor role and then we took our first senior pastoral assignment as a married couple. Larry spent 34 years leading congregations and large staffs from the senior position. Our churches grew large and rapidly. Some remained successful and others failed. He now leads the mission organization that we founded together, Kingdom Global Ministries.

Larry led in our relationship. He took charge of our lives, and I was so grateful that he chose me to follow his calling. He made me no promises except that he would love me, be faithful to me, and that he would keep God's Word as first priority. I didn't know Larry very well when I said, "I do." (Really, I said, "I will.") I will follow your leadership and submit to your headship. Keeping this covenant has proven to be fruitful in my life, although, I am also a leader.

I was seventeen years old and had just graduated from high school when we married. I didn't know that I was a leader, especially in the way that Larry has described me. Yes, I took charge of our household, meticulously caring for our home and family. I accompanied his love for people by providing extraordinary hospitality. Later, I worked in every facet of the church in various seasons where my support was needed. I also worked on jobs outside of the church during seasons of limited income. My attitude was, "Whatever I need to do, I will do." I certainly led in my sphere of influence and responsibility, but at the time, I didn't think of myself as a leader.

Leadership is as varied as the people who fill the lead positions. Leadership also has varied styles. My husband is a strong leader who has an introverted, melancholy temperament. He never seeks to be the life of the party, nor wastes time with trivial pursuits. He carefully plans his strategy to include personal relationships. He is comfortable with solitude and is companioned by meditation. He speaks seldom, but boldly, when he has something to say.

Now, I am a leader too, but one of a different kind, as Larry has clearly described. I am usually noticed when I enter a room. I have to remind myself to take the back seat and not press my way to the front. Solitude for any length of time, for me, is lonely. I speak about any subject as an expert, clearly articulating my point. Sometimes, I really do know what I am talking about, and other times, I will keep you guessing.

People are my life, sort of. Larry spends hours, days, or months with one person at a time. His phone constantly rings with men from across the nation calling "Dad." But me? I like people in groups. So, I create parties: dinner parties, birthday parties, going away parties, or just parties. Who cares what they are for? Larry? He doesn't like parties, but he loves people. I think producing the party is the most enjoyable aspect of the party for me, not the party itself. I love to watch others enjoy something that I have created. I love to share my passions with others, one on one or masses. What I am learning and have learned becomes my platform for teaching others. I will create large venues so others can know what I know—even if that's not much. Radio, television, internet, and crowds of people—the more people I teach, the more people I influence.

WE ARE NOT COMPETITORS

I do not compete with my husband. Titles are not important for either of us. Both of us know where we each excel, and we give one another the release to do just that--excel. We compensate for each other. We are not competitors.

The marked characteristic of a competitor is that they are driven to "win". But when one wins, another loses. Neither Larry nor I try to outdo one another; we promote each other and are one another's cheerleaders. Neither of us wants the other to lose.

SUCCESS IS NOT IN YOUR TITLE

Early in life, we do not fully know what our destination will become. Larry and I have both experienced success together and individually. Our successes are measured more by the influence that we have had in the lives of others, including our children and grandchildren, than by money or material possessions. However, we both have higher visibility reputations because of years of faithful effective ministry and authorships. Our influence has quietly impacted multitudes in nations—together and individually.

Neither of us bears to have earned degrees to give us prestigious titles. Some people value titles and add them to our names out of respect, but we never title ourselves. Titles are not necessary to prove the point that we are leaders. The fruitfulness of whom we lead is the validation that we are effective leaders, not our titles. When you know who you are, you do not have to prove it.

One time, our son gently rebuked me when I introduced him as Dr. Aaron Titus. Although he holds an earned doctorate degree in physics and is an honored university professor and a respected published scientist, he never signs his name or introduces himself using his title. Neither does his wife, Dr. Kimberly Titus, who holds an earned doctorate in Physics. Kim is a university professor of mathematics.

It is only proper for titles to be used within the environment of the earned degree or recognition. For example, on Aaron's university campus, to his students and in his classroom, he is Dr. Titus. However, among his peers and colleagues, he never self-acclaims.

Professional fields do not attach titles of descriptive functions in front of names. For example, we would never write or state, "Please meet Manager Felipe Hasegawa, or this is Director Devi Titus. My medical physician does not have his title on his office door. The sign reads his name, followed by his earned degree symbols. Others may choose to call him "doctor," and he only calls himself "Doc" in his environment of service.

The Bible does not use titles. Biblical text refers to friends, family, and colleagues in ministry by first names: Jesus, Paul, Peter, James, John, Abraham, Isaiah and so on. So why are we so consumed in the church with self-acclaimed titles: Bishop, pastor, co-pastor, elder, prophetess, apostle, evangelist, etc. These can effectively be used as descriptive adjectives, clarifying our function, but not titles, hoping to define our success.

Women who are married to pastors in some Christian affiliations seem to be vulnerable to self-titling and seeking to co-lead. I encourage all women to grow in your individual leadership while supporting your husband's calling and God will give you the recognition that you deserve. You do not have to strive for your significance. No other profession includes giving wives a title to coincide with their spouse's profession; neither should we. In a church denomination where Larry fellowshipped, leaders encouraged me to be ordained. I declined because I had never been to Bible College, let alone Seminary. I love the Holy Scriptures and reading them is a daily part of my life. I now teach the principles that I have learned from the Bible to multitudes. I write books about them and sell CD and DVD's, further multiplying my messages. I minister to others, as all Christians should do, but I do not need a certificate on my wall to validate what I have not earned. If an honorary degree was bestowed on me for my life-achievements, I would consider receiving it, but with a sense of undeserved humility.

> I encourage all women to grow in your individual leadership while supporting your husband's calling and God will give you the recognition that you deserve.

Your degrees, or lack of degrees, do not measure your success.

WHEN SUCCESS KNOCKS AT BOTH OF YOUR DOORS

Truly, neither you nor your spouse was born a leader. You were born babies. The nurse did not look at your mother and say, "Oh, you have just given birth to a leader." However, God had your destiny in mind before the foundations of the earth. You are His idea. He gave you a personality, or temperament, that will define the type of leader you will become. Leaders are developed. It took time for both of you to grow into who you are. You have matured in your personal identity.

When you both have found your passion and live in the fruitfulness of who God created you to be, it is an amazing place to be. Nothing to strive for, compete with or be intimidated by. Seasons in life will flex your focus, but what remains the same is your personal confidence. You are not threatened by your spouse's success—rather, you celebrate it.

Because Larry is a quiet, humble, and strong leader, his success will never put his photo on billboards. However, his faithful years of discipleship to others now keeps his phone ringing daily with, "Hi, Dad" on the other end of the line. Is it possible to have hundred, or thousands of sons? I could have answered, "No," but Larry has proven me wrong.

Larry has successfully grown large churches, trained leaders, started churches and Bible Colleges, and inspired leadership in untold thousands. His influence keeps his phone ringing and his suitcase packed, traveling the world, answering the call of God in his life.

I also am experiencing something that I did not plan. I have been fully satisfied to follow Larry, pack his suitcase, support him, host his multitude of friends and attend to our family. However, God had something else in mind for me—something that I did not plan.

I am successful, too. I have fully supported my husband in all that God has called him to do. I have also raised godly children, begun businesses, launched new ministry venues, and now travel the world and author books that are published in multiple languages. I am a sought-after Christian Women's Conference speaker. In my senior years, I have a high-profile ministry to women. This is not a result of strategic planning or writing pointed mission statements. One by one, I have accepted invitations and now have more than I can personally fulfill. My passion is to *restore the dignity and sanctity of the home* in the way men and women view the home in relationship to the human heart. I am driven to do this with every potential medium of communication that exists. At age sixty-five, I am seeking diligently to learn technology, social media, and newer forms of communication to increase my imprint on today's family, which is in desperate need.

Examine my life and Larry's life. Success has knocked at both of our doors—together and individually. This success gives us new challenges that must be understood and managed in order to keep our relationship flourishing. All leaders share a few things in common and these things must be managed, so you will thrive and not dive.

EMBRACING COMMON LEADERSHIP REALITIES

When you live with a leader, there are some things that cannot be changed. These are common to all leaders and they must be managed. When leaders live together, it doubles the responsibility of leaderships. Embracing, rather than resisting, these realities will allow you to live in harmony. Otherwise, your relationship can end with a cataclysmic collision. Consider these very important realities.

1. *Leaders have time demands.* Schedules and deadlines are all part of the system a leader creates to reach his or her goals. Therefore, a spouse should seek to keep accurate calendars of dates and times, so he or she can approach each day with a feeling of preparedness, rather than chaos.

Communicate daily concerning your schedules and make adjustments for togetherness whenever possible. Don't allow time demands to cause you to lead separate lives.

> This success gives us new challenges that must be understood and managed in order to keep our relationship flourishing.

Larry and I both travel extensively as public speakers. Our audiences are different. I speak to women and he speaks to men and congregations. In this season of success, we are apart a lot. Communicating with one another regarding our schedules, consulting one another before making commitments, and considering one another in the process is very important. It keeps our hearts together and allows us to participate with each other in prayer, concerns, and reports.

It is important to put each other on your calendar. If you do not do this, other requests will squeeze out time for your spouse. It would be senseless for me to constantly complain that Larry is away much of the time. Complaining only makes matters worse for both of you and does not properly communicate what you need to say.

Release your spouse to do what is necessary. But make your time count when you are together. Schedule that time as if it is an unbreakable appointment.

2. *Leaders have followers.* Life with a leader always includes other people. His people and my people can be different. A common way for some to deal with a leader's "other" people is to become possessive and try to limit his or her relationships. Another is to become isolated and remain uninvolved and non-participatory in your spouse's activities. Either of these choices will hinder your relationship and your effective leadership.

Although you must schedule times to be alone with your spouse, the only true solution is to appreciate that your leader has others who are willing to follow. Enjoy participating, as much as possible, in the leadership area of his or her life.

Larry does not like to attend women's conferences. But I have made incredible lifetime friends with some of these women. Now, he spends time with their spouses and us. We enjoy one another's company, because he chose to participate with my "followers".

Likewise, Larry is always telling me how incredible this man or that "son" is, and he wants me to meet them. The truth is, Larry wants me to love those he loves, and I want him to do the same for me.

It is important to attend events and special occasions with your spouse's "people". If your spouse is the leader of an organization or a corporation, you should accompany him/her to their corporate events and meet their "followers".

His people become my people and my people become his people. We support one another by participating with their people.

3. *Leaders are focused.* There is little room for spontaneity when living with a leader. Leaders are focused on their goals; schedules predetermine their activities. When you talk to people who are focused leaders, you usually have only a portion of their attention. Their minds are always preoccupied and their attention span short, much like a child.

Don't take this personally. Use several brief intervals of conversation, rather than trying to keep their attention for a lengthy dissertation. This way, you are more likely to keep your leader's interest.

Larry and I laugh at each other. We can spend hours together and not say one word. We are both focused. He reads; I create. Both require focus. Neither of us complains of being neglected. Remember, he is not a talker and I am a talker. So it is very important that I give him space. But he does the same for me. We do talk; he listens and I talk; we are focused on each other.

Many of our meaningful discussions are regarding our individual revelations, knowledge that we have discovered, and tasks that are at hand. We seek and value one another's opinion. The depths of our convictions come from allowing each other to focus on our passions.

4. *Leaders work with staff.* Leaders are accustomed to giving direction to a group of people, working with them to implement their

vision. They are in authority, and those on their team give input, but seldom question their authority.

Home is different. We are not our spouse's boss. When leaders come home from their work environment, they often continue to treat family as staff, giving assignments and assessments. To keep from doing this, it helps to give a leader time for transition from the work environment to the family environment.

Ladies: your husband is not your personal assistant, your janitor, or your nanny. He is your lover. Do not give him orders when you come home. You can help yourself transition from a task get-it-done environment to a peaceful, loving home mood by creating a soft, warm ambiance—light fragrant candles and play music. Avoid noise and confusion. Speak softly and kindly.

Gentlemen, be just that—gentle. Your wife is not your secretary. She is not your slave. She is not your CFO or your COO. She is your lover. Take off your "leader hat" and put on your "lover hat" when you drive in to your driveway. You are home to be connected, not disconnected. Leave your tasks at work and focus on your tasks at home—your family relationships, beginning with your wife. They are your assignment and your deadline.

5. *Leaders carry stress.* Leadership has stress points that are not always definable. Some things can be talked about, but others are not quite so clear.

Pressures and concerns that cannot be talked about can alter his or her mood. When you notice this is the case, don't nag, trying to find out what is wrong. That only piles on more tension. Help carry the load by being understanding, giving space, and making as many decisions as possible without bothering them with the small stuff. Remember, no situation will last forever. This too will pass. Your loving supportive attitude will relieve their tension and save their health.

There is positive and negative stress. Be sure that you are responsible for managing your own stress points in a positive way. Do not take it out on your spouse, blaming your moodiness on your work situation. You will set the example for them to do the same for you. Remember, you are far from what you once were, but you are not yet where you want to be. Manage your stress in a positive way and build your character.

6. *Leaders can be wrong, too.* Leaders feel such a responsibility to others; it is sometimes difficult for them to accept that they

could be wrong. They may be concerned that their mistake could hurt those whom they are leading. I love and live by my mother's wisdom. She is famous in our family for her sayings and this one is my favorite. "What's so bad about being wrong?" Embracing this attitude frees us from fearing failure and trying to protect ourselves with defensiveness.

Leaders tend to want to cover their mistakes or justify them. Give your leader spouse room to say, "I'm wrong," without fear of criticism. Because you are a solution-finder (leader), it can be your tendency to lecture your spouse when they are discovering and admitting that they are wrong. Be slow to speak, quick to hear, and slow to anger. Your response does wonders for providing the confidence for your spouse to try again.

7. *Leaders need affection.* Give one another lots of affection. Because your leader spouse spends their day with a team of people who support them, work with them, and interrelate in a close way, it is important that they connect with you when they come home. If you are distant and uninterested in them, it will be tempting for them to stay at work and become intimate with another person.

Most leaders are vulnerable to emotional affairs because their spouses do not relate to them in an emotional way. In TRUTH ABOUT CHEATING, author M. Gary Neuman, relationship expert, interviewed 200 men to discover why men cheat. 48% of men rated emotional dissatisfaction as the primary reason they cheated. So much for the myth that for men, cheating is all about sex: Only 8% of men said that sexual dissatisfaction was their reason for cheating.

Express physical connection to your spouse in public when you are in each other's work environments. Greet with a brief kiss, hold hands, a soft pat on their arm or shoulder. This states personal and public affirmation of your relationship. Avoid contradictory statements in public, and protect one another's ego. Speak encouraging, affirming words filled with affection to your spouse's colleagues. State your appreciation for their leadership, accomplishments, and character.

Tickle the tender place in your leader-spouse's heart.

DOUBLE TROUBLE OR DOUBLE REWARD

There is a lot of responsibility in being a leader, and when leaders live together, it can be double trouble or double reward. When Larry is in the limelight, I sit on the front seat, adoring that I get to share in his success. When I am in the limelight, he does the same for me.

Tickle the tender place in your leader-spouse's heart.

Because we work together embracing our challenges rather than resisting the things that we cannot change, we live with a double reward. I love the times we are together, and set him free to be gone as much as is needed. He does the same for me. I am so proud of him and do not have expectations for anything to be different than it is in the moment. Now, in our later years in life, we travel the globe together, speaking as a team--the double reward that has caught us by surprise.

8

[HE Says]

⊙

IT'S MY MONEY, HONEY

By: Larry

Nothing can cause division between marriage partners faster than money. As you might have guessed, in financial matters, as well as everything else, I am totally different than Devi. Is that a set-up for trouble? You bet your bucks, Buddy. As I said before, if I go left, Devi goes right. If I go up, she goes down. If I say yes, she says no. Emphatically! So, when it comes to finances, couples face a great potential of division, especially when both partners have strong personalities, strong opinions and strong incomes.

You can see a real difference between Devi and me when we sell our products. As quickly as Devi sells books, CDs and DVDs from her products table, which on most weekends is quite fast, I'm on the opposite side of the table giving them away just as fast. In fact, if you want to pay the market price for a book, go to Devi. If you want a free book, CD, or DVD, come and see me. She will love you, hug you, sign your book and take your money. I will hug you, give you a squeeze, compliment you, then give you the book free or give your money back. And this is only one of the many ways in which we see and respond to financial situations differently.

Could you ever have imagined that differences in your childhood backgrounds would impact your marriage in such an influential way? Marriage can exacerbate many issues, and money sits at the top of the list.

As a child, my parents never taught me to save money. Now, as an adult, it's still hard for me to save. No one taught me how to manage my money or how to budget. I don't remember one time my parents ever teaching me about finances, other than that I should tithe. We didn't have credit cards back then, but if I did, I would have been up to my eyeballs in debt. As it was, I waited until several years of marriage before I got up to my eyeballs in debt. Maybe my brothers did, but as the last of the siblings, I never knew when my parents weren't struggling financially. We didn't live dirt poor, but Dad never had enough money to quite make it and definitely didn't have enough money to retire. If my Mom hadn't gone to work in the ministry after my dad's stroke, I have no idea how they would have survived.

To this day, I struggle with issues of finances. If I see something I like, I buy it, then and there. I think that's called "instant gratification." I also like the best of whatever it is, and I'm unwilling to take second best. If Devi sees something she likes, she waits until it goes on sale or opts for something that looks just as good, but costs less.

On the other hand, Devi's family lived as hard workers, frugal savers and great money managers. They never made a lot of money, but they saved through the years and eventually retired to a very comfortable living. As for me, I will probably retire sometime after my kids retire. (Thank God they've done away with debtor's prison.)

When Devi and I got married, I had a habit of spending money as soon as I earned it. But now that we've been married for forty-eight years, as soon as the money comes in, it doesn't go out for at least a month. Just kidding, sort of. We're doing better these days, but I have learned to lean more heavily on Devi's wisdom than my emotions, including my need of instant gratification or wanting to "bless" someone. She's not shy about saying, "Honey, you shouldn't give that person money. They haven't worked for it. It's not good for them." What can I say? I just love blessing people. But I still need to remember that sometimes blessing people becomes a detriment to their learning and hence, not a blessing, but a hindrance to their growth.

Money and finances present a unique opportunity for couples to either bond in a mutual goal or divide over differing opinions and directions. The divisions may not only run deep, but can also lead to fissures that don't heal over time. Many marriages have fallen through the cracks of differing or intransigent opinions on financial matters, ending either in divorce or a great divide of disunity that lasts for years.

It's rare, but some couples have similar backgrounds when it comes to finances; they have both learned to effectively manage money, and they share similar opinions regarding financial decisions. If you're one of those couples, congratulations! You're part of the elite and probably one of the 144,000 in Revelation 7. (Just kidding)

However, not every husband or wife has had the blessing of learning financial management from their parents during their formative years. Most likely, only one of you has had the opportunity to bring into your marriage sage financial advice from your childhood.

It wouldn't be uncommon, in such cases, for the trained spouse to feel that the other is either immature, irresponsible, or at least naïve when it comes to financial decisions. Though that would be true, it does little good to approach the issue with any type of condescending attitude. Harboring bitterness or haranguing a weak spouse will never improve the marriage relationship or heal the financial woes. Encouragement, affirmation and love can cover a multitude of financial sins and mistakes.

In many cases, both spouses enter the marriage without a clue of how to save or manage their money. Wow! Disaster waits at the door unless the couple takes action immediately. Marriage counseling can really help if it's done in advance.

What about your fiscal gifts or expertise? In many, if not most, cases, one of the marriage partners will have more knowledge and expertise about money management than the other. For example, a good number of men have success investing in the stock market. In addition, the wife often has proficient accounting skills, while the husband works hard to make the money for her to skillfully manage. In some marriages, it's the reverse. It's just critical that you find which one of you does what, best. Then, let that person take over that responsibility, the sooner the better.

To me, the most important principle of all is that you come into agreement before making any major decision. This is especially true in finances. God loves unity. God wants you to live unified. It is more important that you be unified than that you be right. At least you'll be wrong together.

It has taken Devi and me years to figure out how to best handle our finances. Or maybe I should say it has taken me years to figure out that Devi has a better financial head, and I just have a stubborn head.

Devi sees the big picture. Financial management and saving money comes very natural to her. I have found out, through many years of trial and error, that in all negotiations, I had better let her lead the way. When purchasing a car, home, appliance, or planning for the future, she always stays light-years ahead of me. It is always a disaster if I make the decision unilaterally. When purchasing a car, I'm shocked I haven't offered a shyster car dealer extra money if he would just let me buy his car for additional money over the sticker price. I just want to please everyone and make others happy.

But when it comes to the check-book, however, hand it over to me, baby. Her sanguine personality seems to kick in at the checkout counter. She might write the date on the amount line of the check, or the previous check amount on the current check, or forget to write anything in the check register. It always gives us a reason to laugh, cry or celebrate when I open up the monthly bank statement. "Honey, where did this check come from? What's this amount? Honey, we're overdrawn. Honey, we've got an extra $1,000 this month because you forgot to write in the deposit." We either cry, "Help!" or "Hallelujah!"

It should be a no-brainer—discover each other's expertise and turn it over to them. And, men especially, don't try to control your finances if that's not your gift. Admit it, get over it, and turn over your check book to the one God knew could keep you financially solvent, organized, and looking smarter than you actually are.

Before you skim through my chapter thinking, "This guy is a total financial dud," hold on. I may be a financial dud, but I'm a much better financial dud than I used to be. Before attaching the moniker, "Financial Dud!" to my name, you should know about some of my better qualities:

+ I never discourage my wife from dreaming and saving for her dream. I've heard so many guys respond to a wife's plea for a better dishwasher, sofa, bed or home, with a curt, "We can't afford it." What a way to kill a dream. Encourage her dream by beginning a savings account, or working an extra job or extra hours to save money, but don't kill her dream.

+ Make sure that she has money in her handbag at all times, without her having to beg for it. If you're down to your last dollar, give it to her. When you get cash out of the bank, give her half of it; after all, she's half of you.

+ I consider all of "my" money to be hers as well. I have never earned a dollar that I've wanted to keep for myself and not share with her. Don't consider your money "yours," but "ours." We're in this together. Everything is "ours—" our children, our home, our money, our dreams and, yes, our debts.

+ I tithe and give the first ten percent of everything I ever make to God's Kingdom and church. God might adjudicate a number of things as being deficient on my account when we meet on judgment day, but when it comes to tithing, I never rob God.

+ I always pay my bills on time. I do have to make a few exceptions, like when I don't have any money because I purchased something I couldn't afford, but these are rare exceptions.

+ I do not make eternal decisions based on financial considerations.

Lastly, people may ask the question, "If my wife works, do we share that money or is it hers?" That demands a brilliant answer. For that reason, I will gladly defer and pass the question on to my wife. See how submissive I am?

8

[SHE Says]

IT'S MY MONEY, HONEY

By: Devi

YES, LARRY AND I grew up with very different views of money. When I was young, my Dad worked as a non-union butcher, cutting meat in the small town grocery store that his nephew owned. He did not make much money. My mother worked as a clerk in the same small grocery store during the months that we attended school. In the summer, she stayed home with us and drew unemployment. Later, my mother became the postmaster of our small town post office, and Daddy became the pastor of our small church. They both retired from these positions. I was in high school when mother began her postal work and just married when Daddy became the pastor of the church that I grew up attending.

We did not see ourselves as poor, but according to government charts, we were. I dressed in fashionable and lovely clothing because mother sewed most of what I wore. In fact, I considered myself one of the best-dressed girls in school. We also kept our furniture updated, and our home, although it was 100 years old, remained among the nicest in our small rural town of 300 people.

My brother, who is four years older than I, began working in the stock room of the same store when he was quite young. I took care of the house, set the table, and started our dinner meal before mother came home each day. I was employed with my first paying job at fifteen, as soon as I got my driver's license. However, I was twelve years old when I began earning money. I took in ironing and also worked as the town "beautician" for my mother's friends and relatives. I did really well with the roller sets and teasing hair. The styles that I created lasted one week until ready for another shampoo and set. The money that I earned was *my* money. I saved much of it and spent some of it.

On Saturdays, my brother and I got to sleep in until 8:00am! After morning chores, our parents let us play in the afternoon. Our chores consisted of housework, mowing and hoeing weeds outside. He and I shared and exchanged work assignments, just to keep life interesting. I had never heard of someone

84

receiving an allowance until I got to high school. My comment to my friend was, "You mean your parents just give you money without you working for it?" It seemed ridiculous.

I remember so well my Dad opening his wallet to show me two hidden compartments. One was designated for his tithe, ten percent of his paycheck, which he cashed weekly. He set aside this tithe to give to the church. The other was designated for one-fourth of our monthly house payment. Each week, Daddy put the allotted cash in these compartments to make sure he didn't spend it on other things. This example made an indelible impression on me. Credit simply was not used in our household, and I did not even know it existed until shortly before I married.

My family got into a pattern of earning money, saving it, sharing it, and spending some of it. With the savings that Mom and Dad accumulated, they later purchased a few rentals, which produced a good supplemental and retirement income.

Because Larry and I married very young, we did not discuss our values regarding money. Let me explain our personalities for a moment, so you can understand our challenges in how we handle money. I am visionary, determined, decisive and very task oriented; Larry is stable, loyal, dependable, easy going, and very people oriented. I tend to want to control people and situations, and Larry has a stubborn personality at times. You can easily see that our strengths work very well together, but our weaknesses have the potential to poison and destroy our relationship.

Early in our marriage, we did like most people; we bounced back and forth several times with who pays the monthly bills and manages the household expenses. When I paid the bills, I treated Larry like a child. I gave him an allowance and said no to his spending patterns more often than I said yes. I manipulated our money, took risks, and did not make payments on time. This demeaned his manhood and his sense of fulfillment as our provider. When I turned everything over to him, I did not trust that we would ever own anything. I thought he would give everything away, and I feared we would have nothing left for our family.

Neither he nor I had a clue about making a budget and sticking to it. We just earned money, seemingly never enough, and spent what we earned. We thought we were working together, but in reality, I shut down and did not express my opinions when he took charge—a setup for a future financial train wreck!

Making a budget with projected income and expenses didn't work for us because, unlike most people, we did not know how much we were going to earn each week. In our generation of ministry, most of our income came from "love offerings," which gave us barely enough to survive. When we did earn a meager salary, we usually did not receive it on time.

Tension and conflict ensued in this kind of financial environment. Larry was too generous; he gave everything away, including the equity of our second home and cars that were not paid for. Because I trusted Larry's spirituality more than I trusted mine, I was afraid to interfere. I thought that my selfishness and lack of abandon faith would cause us to not have God's provision, anointing and blessing in our lives. So, I kept silent.

After several years, I realized that I had responsibility, not for our money, but for my heart. No matter how we spent our money or how much debt occurred, I knew that I could not let resentment reside in my heart, nor could I allow this difference to become a wedge in our relationship.

I settled in my heart before God that whether rich or poor, whatever our financial outcome would be due to poor management or good management, I would remain content. I would live in love, peace, and harmony with Larry, whether in the ghetto or a suburb neighborhood. I would fully relinquish control and trust my husband and the Lord for our future welfare.

I have always earned money in some way or another during our marriage. I am naturally entrepreneurial and read in Proverbs 31 that a virtuous woman, when she cares for her husband and family, can also earn money. This is what I did and still do today.

I have released control of all finances, and Larry has taken charge. I came up with this idea. I give him what I earn. He deposits it in our joint account. My money is his. His money is mine. He pays the bills and keeps my wallet filled with cash, if we have any. He remains generous with me, and when I desire to make a personal purchase of significant expense, I always call him. I do this out of respect, not out of obligation. He never requires me to ask his permission to spend money, but when I ask permission, this gives me accountability so I do not spend impulsively. It also keeps us connected and informed with one another's desires and choices.

Checking in with him and him with me also keeps us blended in our relationship and in our interests. It keeps us living interdependently rather than independently.

My money is his. His money is mine.

Because I trusted Larry and released control, Larry has actually become a very good manager. We still live by faith, but lack nothing. Together, we have climbed nearly out of debt, and he remains vigilant to keep us on track with timely payments, savings and all of the things that we should have done when we were younger.

We do not look back in regret and blame. God provided for us prosperity, but we wasted some of it. However, we are facing our senior years with something more important than stocks and bonds and big bank accounts. We live in harmony, love, and unity. This relationship has given us the joy of a loving family with strong godly character who works out their challenges in life and stays committed to their marriages. We now also enjoy sitting on the sidelines watching our adult grandchildren figure out in a quicker way the things that took us years to discover. Will we leave an inheritance to our family? Yes; it will not be as much as it could have been had we better managed our money, but that is okay with all of us. The values learned from these life-lessons greatly enrich their lives.

The generational inheritance promised by God to Abraham includes transferring five essential elements to generations to come. They include the *faith* that Abraham had in God and the *provision* that God gave Abraham. Abraham was a good steward of that provision; therefore, it multiplied and became *prosperity*. Abraham remained radically obedient and that *obedience* led him into an *intimate relationship with God*. This is the promise of the inheritance that can be passed to our generations. Although our bank account that will transfer to our children at the end of our days will not be enough to sustain them, their *inheritance* includes so much more.

We have passed to them faith, provision, prosperity (to a small degree), obedience, and intimacy with God. What more could a family desire? And our greatest reward is seeing our children transfer these values to their children, and our adult grandchildren training their children in the same ways that my parents trained me.

Larry has taught me how to share generously the things that God has given us and to trust Him with our lives. I have demonstrated to him the rich life of frugality and creativity. Releasing one another allows both of us to experience our common love of beauty—a beautiful home and a beautiful life. We now share the joy of giving, saving and spending—a miracle for both of us.

9

[HE Says]

⟳

WE'RE SO DIFFERENT

By: Larry

U NITY IS NEVER sameness or oneness. Unity requires diversity. I can't be one with myself. I can only be one with someone else and that other person must be totally different for us to achieve unity. To even say, "We are so different, we should have never married," is absurd. It's precisely because you are so different that unity can be attained. If God were interested in "oneness," He would not have extricated Eve from the side of Adam. Because Eve was removed from the "side" of Adam, then physiologically, women are going to be different than men.

In marriage, God requires that two completely different people become one. *"For this reason a man will leave his father and mother and be united to his wife, and they will become one flesh."* This verse, first mentioned by God in Genesis 2:24 (NIV), is so important that it's repeated again in the New Testament by Jesus in Matthew 19:5 and Mark 10:7-8, and by Paul in I Corinthians 6:16. It is God's idea, then, that two totally different people should become one flesh.

Unity requires diversity.

Of course, everyone is already aware of the enormous differences between men and women as a gender; she likes company, he likes caves; she likes shopping, he likes sports; she likes gourmet food, he likes greasy gravy; she likes to dress up, he likes jeans and a T-shirt; she likes to ask endless questions, he answers in just a few mono-syllabic grunts; she can tell her innermost thoughts to the cashier at the grocery market in front of God and everyone, he won't share his secrets with a deaf priest in a confessional booth; she spends hours getting ready, he brushes his teeth and is out the door; she's always cold, he's always hot.

As an aside, I would highly recommend the book or DVD series called

Marriage on the Rock, by Jimmy Evans, for an outstanding treatment on this subject. He teaches on how diversity should help, rather than hinder, marriage relationships. I'm admittedly biased, since Jimmy and Karen remain my close friends, but I have never, ever heard better or more practical teaching on marriage than comes from Jimmy. Go to Amazon and order this series before reading the rest of this chapter. You'll be glad you did—it can save your marriage.

The other day, I was watching four teenagers standing on a corner with car wash signs, trying to coax customers to come in and purchase a car wash for their fund raising project. Actually, I should say, three teenagers standing with signs and one teenager sitting with the sign on his lap. The three standing teenagers were girls and the fourth one, sitting down, was the boy. Does that tell you anything about the genders? Three girls yelling, screaming, waving their signs at every car that passed by, and one boy sitting on the bench with the sign on his lap, picking his nose. And they're not even married yet. If they were married, he would be lying down with the sign covering his eyes from the sun, his slurpy melting nearby.

On every page of this book, you've read about our different perspectives—on everything.

In the animal world, I describe Devi as the Cheetah and me as the three-toed sloth. Please understand, however, that I'm the three-toed, not the two-toed sloth, which is totally unacceptable as well as downright insulting. That one extra toe makes all the difference in the world.

The Cheetah can sprint from seventy to seventy-five miles per hour. It can accelerate from zero to sixty-five miles per hour in just three seconds. And I, the three-toed sloth, on the other hand, can reach speeds of up to 0.15 miles per hour, when I'm in a hurry, that is. That's why one extra toe comes in handy when you're in a rush. I sleep nearly all day long, hanging upside down. I eat upside down, and also have "you-know-what" upside down, which is no easy trick. I do everything upside down (Do you feel sorry for Devi yet?). I can barely finish this paragraph without wanting to go and take a nap. Does that describe me or what? I laugh at myself because it's better than crying. If I were to cry upside down, I would risk drowning.

How do two people so diverse become unified? How can two total opposites work in unity? Or, to reverse that last sentence, how can two people come into unity without work?

First, I want you to know the importance that the Bible places on unity.

Jesus' last prayer, found in John 17, was that His church, His body, would become one.

Why did Jesus consider unity so important? The answer is found in John 10, 14, and 17. Let me get a little theological on you. Simply put, Jesus and the Father are unified, and He wants that for His kids. On the flip side, the devil does everything he can to destroy unity; the devil loves division, hatred, malice, selfishness and divorce.

In John 10:30, Jesus declares that He and the Father are one. The Greek word for one is "hice" and it means one in purpose, not in person. It would have been impossible for Jesus and the Father to be one if They were the same person because unity demands diversity. Throughout the Bible, Jesus and the Father fill two completely different roles:

THE PERSON OF JESUS, THE SON

- Jesus describes Himself as the Son and God as His Father (John 5:17, 19 ff; I John 1:3).
- Jesus is seated at the right hand of the Father (Romans 8:34; I John 2:1; Ephesians 1:20; Hebrews 1:3).
- Jesus doesn't know the date of His return, only the Father knows (Matthew 24:36).
- Jesus came to do the will of the Father, not His own will (John 4:34; 5:19; 9:4; Luke 22:42).
- Jesus prayed to the Father, not vice-versa, and He requests that we do the same (Matthew 6:6-14; John 17).
- Jesus didn't speak His own words, do His own miracles, or make His own judgments (John 5:19-30; 6:38; 7:16; 8:28).
- Jesus will take the completed Kingdom of God and give it to the Father (I Corinthians 15:24-28).
- Jesus created the heavens and the earth according to His Father's plan (Hebrews 1:2; 11:3; Colossians 1:15-18).
- Jesus died on the cross; the Father did not (Matthew, Mark, Luke, John).
- Jesus came with the full nature of the Father to live in human flesh. The Father did not come to live in the flesh (John 1:14; Philippians 2:6; Colossians 1:19; 2:9,10).

+ Jesus was mortal. The Father is the only One who dwells in immortality (I Timothy 1:17; 6:16; Luke 24:39; I John 1:1).
+ Jesus bore the sins of the world. The Father did not (II Corinthians 5:21; I Peter 2:24).
+ Jesus is the Mediator; the Father is the Goal (Acts 4:12; I Timothy 2:5).
+ Jesus has a spiritual Body called the Church. The Father does not (I Corinthians 12:13, 18, 28).
+ Jesus is returning on a white horse to judge the nations of the world. The Father is not (Revelation 19:11).
+ Jesus had a physical body that multitudes saw and touched. No one has ever seen the Father (John 1:18; Colossians 1:15; I John 1:1; Luke 24:39; I Timothy 6:16).
+ Jesus came from the Father to this earth, not vice-versa (John 1:14).
+ Jesus is the Messiah, the Christ; the Father is not (Matthew 1:16; 16:16; John 1:45).
+ Jesus receives worship because He redeemed people with His blood (Revelation 5). The Father receives worship because He created all things (Revelation 4).
+ Jesus was sent from the Father; the Father was never sent from Jesus (John 17:18; 20:21).

THE PERSON OF THE FATHER

+ The Father spoke from heaven on three occasions to the Son who was on earth (Luke 3:22; 9:35; John 12:28).
+ The Father's throne and home are in heaven (Matthew 6:1, 9).
+ The Father has an Only Begotten Son, Jesus. Though God has many sons, only Jesus is the Only Begotten of the Father (John 1:14, 18; 3:16; Acts 13:33; I John 4:9).
+ The Father's Throne in heaven is always central, and the Son is always at His right hand (Revelations 4 & 5; 22:1; Psalms 110:1; Ephesians 1:20-22).
+ The Father appointed Jesus the Heir of all things and through Him created the universe (Hebrews 1:1, 2).

+ The Father gave His fullness to Jesus, not vice-versa (Colossians 1:19; 2:9).

+ The Father is Spirit (John 4:24). Spirits do not have flesh and bone (Luke 24:39).

+ The Father has never been seen by man, nor can man see Him and live (I Timothy 1:17; 6:16; Exodus 33:20; John 1:18; 6:46).

+ The Father is the One who draws people to the Son (John 6:44; John 17:2).

+ The Father gave His glory to the Son (John 17:5, 24).

+ The Father sent the Son into the world (John 17:18).

+ The Father is invisible (Colossians 1:15; I Timothy 1:17; 6:16; John 1:18).

+ The Father is greater than all (John 10:29; 14:28).

+ The Father commanded the Son, but the Son never commanded the Father (John 14:31).

+ The Father put everything under the feet of Christ (I Corinthians 15:27; Ephesians 1:22; Psalms 8:6; 110:1; Matthew 22:44).

+ The Father will receive all the Kingdoms of the world from Jesus; Jesus will then submit Himself to the Father that the Father may be "all in all" (I Corinthians 15:28).

+ The Father gave the Son a name, a title, that is above every other name or title (Ephesians 1:21; Philippians 2:9-11).

+ The Father raised Jesus from the dead (Ephesians 1:19, 20; Galatians 1:1).

+ The Father is immortal. The Son experienced mortality, or death (I Timothy 1:17; 6:16).

+ The Father reconciled the world to Himself in Christ (I Corinthians 5:19).

+ The Father will tabernacle, or dwell, among us in the New Jerusalem as Jesus dwelt among the disciples 2,000 years ago (Revelation 21:3).

+ The Father dwells in unapproachable light. Jesus, the Light of the World, was easily approached (I Timothy 5:16; I John 1:1).

And this is only a partial list of the differences between the Father and His Only Begotten Son, Jesus. The reason I show you these scriptures is to point out that Jesus and the Father are two completely different personalities (persons), but are totally one, unified in purpose.

In John 10:38, Jesus describes how their diversity allows Them to achieve unity. *Understand that the Father is in me and I am in the Father.* In John 14:10, Jesus says, *"Don't you believe that I am in the Father, and that the Father is in me? The words that I say to you I do not speak on my own authority, but the Father who dwells in me does his works. Believe me that I am in the Father and the Father is in me, or else believe on account of the works themselves."* In verse 23 of the same chapter, Jesus says, *"If anyone loves me, he will keep my word, and my Father will love him, and we will come to him and make our home with him."*

In John 17:21, Jesus broadens His explanation of unity to include the believer as well: *"That they may all be one, just as you, Father, are in me, and I in you."* In verse 22, He amplifies it by saying, *"The glory that you have given me I have given to them, that they may be one even as we are one."* Now, verse 23 is the clincher, wrapping it all up: *"I in them and you in me, that they may become perfectly one, so that the world may know that you sent me and loved them even as you loved me."*

It is important to now apply this to marriage because God commands that we, husband and wife, become one, just like Jesus and the Church are one. *"Therefore a man shall leave his father and mother and hold fast to his wife, and the two (Greek "duo") shall become one (Greek "hice") flesh. This mystery is profound, and I am saying that it refers to Christ and the church"* (Ephesians 5:31-32).

Notice that in all cases, the personalities involved never become the other person, but their personalities blend together when the uniting parties make the deliberate choice to do so.

I want to give you a simple, but profound, illustration. When you were born again, two things happened as it related to you and Jesus. Jesus spiritually took up residence inside you, and you spiritually took up residence inside Him. The Holy Spirit accomplished this process because of your decision to accept Christ (See I Corinthians 12:13). You didn't become Jesus and He didn't become you. You just began living inside each other in a spirit of unity, in the same way that the Father lives in the Son and the Son lives in the Father. Paul says, in several passages, that we are *in* Christ. He also says that Christ lives *in* us. Which is true? Both are true. The two, Jesus and you, have become one. Does that sound like something you would want in your marriage?

93

As a quick excursion, Paul goes to length in verses 3 and 13 of Ephesians 4 to emphasize that unity is demanded not just for married couples, but for the entire Body of Christ.

(Be) eager to maintain the unity of the Spirit in the bond of peace. Ephesians 4:3.

Until we all attain to the unity of the faith. Ephesians 4:13.

Here is the bottom line: Either we come into unity with God the Father, Jesus Christ, our spouses, and with our fellow brothers and sisters or we are patently out of the will of God.

It grieves me to see so many married couples living separate lives, never coming into unity, never living as one with each other and one in Christ. Unless you live in unity, you remain married in name only.

Paul goes to lengths in several New Testament passages to emphasize the importance of unity. *"Make every effort to keep the unity of the Spirit through the bond of peace,"* he pleads in Ephesians 4:3. *"Make every effort"* is the English translation of the Greek word *"spoudazo,"* which means to *"make haste, be zealous, and be speedy."* In the Titus translation, it means, "hurry up!" Understand the importance of unity, and then do all in your power to produce it immediately in your marriage. It's a BIG DEAL!

> Unless you live in unity, you remain married in name only.

When Jesus says that He and the Father are one in John 10:30, it doesn't mean sameness, but oneness in diversity. The proof of this is in the previous verse where Jesus describes the Father as being greater than He (See also John 14:28). Jesus, according to Paul's description of Him in Philippians 2:5-10, had already divested Himself of the privileges of equality with the Father when He came to incarnate Himself as God/man on this earth. So, any attempt to make "oneness" mean "sameness" already falls flat. Unity requires diversity, and next to Jesus and the Church, God the Father and God the Son, marriage is a perfect example of how diverse people can become *one*. In fact, other than Deity, marriage is the best example of unity that the Bible gives us.

If I were to amplify and exposit the rest of the verses and chapters on unity in the Bible, it would require that I write a whole new book on just this one topic, which I don't intend to do, at least not now. But, suffice it to say, unity is a big deal in the Bible. In fact, it appears, if one were to believe the dismal statistics on marriage, it's a much bigger deal than married couples realize. Do we really understand how much God values unity, and do we *"make every effort to keep the unity of the Spirit through the bond of peace?"*

You cannot produce a symphony using one instrument. Harmony requires several distinct instruments. Neither can we build marriages and maintain them without the harmony of diversity.

Here are some suggestions for maintaining unity in your marriage:

+ Both of you need to clearly understand that the man is the head of the marriage. Authority, which is what headship provides, always precedes unity. This remains not only true in marriage, but in every other aspect of civilized society. At every event you attend, someone is in charge and others have to defer to their wishes.

    If there is not a clear understanding of headship, there will never be unity in the marriage, in the church, in the corporation, in the nation, in the army, or anywhere else. So, let me ask you a basic, yet profound, question: Who is the head in your marriage? If the answer is you, the man, then we can go on to the next point. If your answer is not the man, then there can be no unity until that choice, and it is a choice, is made by both spouses.

+ Choose to honor and prefer the other spouse. Selfishness will destroy a marriage; putting the other first will produce unity and selflessness. Refer to Philippians 2:5-10 to see how Jesus did this. The question always comes, but aren't we both equal? Of course you are, just as Jesus and the Father are equal, but Jesus chose to humble Himself instead of demanding equality. Both spouses must make this same choice; you must humble yourself and not demand your own way (See I Peter 3:7).

> Selfishness will destroy a marriage; putting the other first will produce unity and selflessness.

+ Enjoy, rather than despise, your diversity. Though I referred to this at length in Chapter Two, I want to include it again, as a point of reminder. There can be no unity as long as you despise the beauty of diversity. God made you different then brought you together to function as one. That cute little thing that sat beside you while you were courting is still the cute little thing she was then, but you now despise what you once thought was cute. So, who's changed? Love her diversity. Thank God she doesn't act like you.

+ Learn how to defer and submit to one another. It's true that in Ephesians 5:22 Paul tells women to submit to men. But, in the previous verse, he enjoins us to submit to one another. I think that "one another" might include both of you; what do you think?

> Enjoy, rather than despise, your diversity.

If you will submit more to your wife, you might find out that God speaks to her more often than you think. And it will keep you from making a lot of stupid mistakes that you will most likely make if you don't listen.

+ Do things together. Sit together; hold hands together; walk together; go to appointments together; ride together (that sounds ludicrous, but in this age of multiple vehicles, couples can spend days and weeks riding in separate vehicles); go to sporting events together; watch TV together and for heaven's sake, eat together. By the way, Devi has an excellent book on this called *The Table Experience*.

Honestly, I would rather have a root canal than go shopping with my wife. But, for the sake of being together, I carry along a book and look for the nearest chair in the "lingerie" department.

Find ways to be together when you're not together, such as:

+ Call her during the day or night.
+ E-mail, text, or write her "love" notes.
+ Talk to others about her, extolling her virtues.
+ Delay major decisions until you can "talk it through."

It not only takes two to tango, it takes two to become one, and if God commanded it, then let's get with it.

9

[SHE Says]

◐

WE'RE SO DIFFERENT

By: Devi

ARRY HAS EXTENSIVELY expressed how different we are. It is interesting for me to read about our differences from his perspective. Because, from my perspective, they do not seem to be so exaggerated. Perhaps it is because I view him as "different" and me as "normal." When you view something in perspective, your nearside will be his far side and vice-versa, although you are viewing the same things.

Understanding this helps you realize one of the values of unity: unity expands each person's viewpoint. What you see as most important (your near side) and what he sees as most important (his near side) could be the same thing from two different angles. When you unite your different perspectives, you get a more complete view than you would have by yourself.

Ask yourself this ultimate question: Are you willing to unify in your diversity? Chapter two helps you to appreciate your differences and to celebrate them. But, to unify is altogether a different thing.

The word *unify* is a verb and not a noun—it describes the process of working toward the goal of unity. For two to become one is a state of being: Unity. However, to embrace the process of unification is to embrace a journey of self-sacrifice and self-awareness. It is impossible to achieve unity if two people remain unwilling to unify.

Now, let's discuss this journey of unification. Think of two roads coming from two very different communities. One perhaps comes from a small country town and the other from a metropolitan city. At some point, these two roads merge into an interstate highway. Neither of these two roads, on their own, can take you to a multitude of interesting places without merging, leaving behind their points of origin for the sake of reaching a new destination.

When leaders marry, they are both qualified and even experienced from two different worlds. It would be great if we could say that unity automatically happens on the wedding night. But, that is not true. What does happen, though, is that each person begins the journey of moving from their pasts to their future together. Notice that "pasts" is plural and "future" is singular.

> To embrace the process of unification is to embrace a journey of self-sacrifice and self-awareness.

Too often, tragically, couples live their lives with two futures, each going their own way and doing their own thing. Unfortunately, this kind of living is only half as fulfilling as living a life of unity—fully embracing one another's passions, interests, and achievements. Back to the analogy—oftentimes, when the individual two-lane roads merge together, they become a six or eight lane highway, not merely a four-lane road.

The blending process of two very different people from two very different backgrounds can be uncomfortable, but don't give up. With practice, you get better at blending your lives and living in unity. Just keep thinking about the eight-lane highway that your lives can form together. At times, you drive in the same lane, and at other times, you each drive in your own lane, but you always know which lane each of you are in and where you are going together.

Let's consider the essential components to unity: Self-Sacrifice and Self Awareness.

Self-Sacrifice: Give one another freedom to fully express yourselves within your personalities. Do not hinder each other. In order to do this, you must sacrifice your personal tastes and preferences in order to allow your spouse to fully express his or hers. It is a truism that our tastes and preferences change over time because of maturity, education, and exposure. Therefore, it becomes limiting to insist that your life partner have the same tastes that you do. So, how do two people unify when they want two very different things? The stronger personality of the two should yield his or her preferences to the softer spoken. When the timid person is free to fully express his or her personal creativity without fear of criticism or ridicule, you will surprisingly discover some new qualities in them that you will love. Stop restricting your partner and enjoy his or her new-found freedom.

You may ask, "But what if I really do not like what the other person likes, such as food, décor, hobbies, interests, etc.?" My response is, "Do you love him or her?" If so, you will sacrifice your "likes" for her pleasure. Notice that I am advising males to do this for their wives. This is where biblical responsibility and gender roles come into play. The husband, who is the head of his wife, is to love her as Christ loves the church. God calls him to lead the way of living self-sacrificially with his wife. His godly headship will release and not restrict his wife. She will be released in her personality and her creativity, which is part of God's nature in her. She will feel safe because of his support.

God makes a clear distinction concerning gender roles. The husband rules the environment in the "field," and the wife rules the environment in the "home." Her freedom of expression must have liberty in the home, and his freedom of expression must have liberty in the type of work he chooses to do. For example, the wife does not encourage her husband to go to medical school when he wants to start a landscape business. She should fully support him in his passion and the profession that he chooses. Neither should he restrict her from rearranging the furniture in the home. Because God has assigned the woman to be the "keeper of the home," she has a responsibility under God to appoint the home and manage it with peace and love. God has given her the responsibility of maintaining the home atmosphere. There is nothing worse than having responsibility and no authority. Therefore, the husband must submit to God and release his wife to create within the home that which she is responsible for. This will energize her in a greater way to care for the home. She must be given freedom to spontaneously move furniture and accessories as she wills without fear or criticism from her husband. Husbands can help and give input, but they must not dominate this environment in the same way she does not dominate him in his work environment.

When a couple supports one another, each person gets better at what they do. The wife, who wanted more for her husband than mowing lawns, could start encouraging him to improve his business skills to grow a large and successful company. The encouraging artistic husband, who wants a well appointed home, can motivate his wife to learn design techniques through research and experimentation to help her grow in her gifting.

We uphold a responsibility to sacrifice our preferences in order to give full release to our partner and unify with his or her choices. The benefit of unifying with the other person is that they will then desire to please you and will ask you for your opinion. The heart of love will desire to include the desire of your spouse. In other words, freedom releases individuality, and love blends tastes, interests and preferences. It's a wonderful way to live.

Self-Awareness: It is impossible to unify with another person who refuses to unify with you. Consider the example of oil and vinegar. They appear unified when you pour them together and shake them up, but given time, they

99

separate again. However, if you add a dab of mustard, an emulsifier, to the oil and vinegar and shake them together, they will never separate. If you, the oil, refuse the wise counsel (addition) of the emulsifier, you can never blend with your vinegar. You can insist on being the way you are and remain an emotional island to yourself. However, if you will admit that you need help—you are not all that you think you are anyway—and hear what others have to say about you, your self awareness will embrace wise counsel that will help you blend with your partner.

> It is impossible to unify with another person who refuses to unify with you.

Laughing about your limitations is the most freeing thing that you can do. It is much better than others laughing at you! Be the first to confess your challenges and the obstacles that hinder you from the pleasures of unity. Talk about your own limitations, and do not talk about the limitations of your partner. This self-awareness frees you from the straightjacket of self-perceived perfectionism. Others quickly recognize your shortcomings, and if you do not admit them, you emotionally isolate yourself from the people you love. And no longer do you receive the respect that you need.

Pride goes before a fall. Pride sets one up for failure. Too many wonderful people have married and failed because they refused to humble themselves. No matter what you think you are good at, there will always be someone better than you that you can learn from. Humble yourself and inquire from your spouse first. When he or she has absolute freedom to speak to you in love and without fear, you will be surprised to discover the wisdom that he or she can give you. In marriage, fear of failure becomes our failure. Performance and perfectionism keep us from our goal—unity.

Humility, however, sets the stage for success. Two humble people, who esteem the uniqueness of each other, are two people who live in the benefits of unity. Joy, laughter, pleasure, sharing, supporting, encouraging, working, and serving together— these are the benefits of unity.

GOOD HABITS OF LIVING IN UNITY

When a couple blends their lives in unity, it will change their habits. Here are a few habits to consider.

1. **Do things together.** The best advice that my parents gave me
when I married was, "Do things together." If he washes the car,
either help him or do another outdoor project at the same time
so you can spend time together. When you cook or clean the
kitchen, do it together. Go to bed together. Get up together.
Make the bed together. Clean the house together. Organize the
garage together. When in a public place, sit together. Do not put
your children between you.

Several years ago, Larry and I cut our budget by driving one car. We
thought that we could do this for six months, and now, ten years later, we still
have only one car. We love the togetherness that it creates. We discovered that
driving one car forces us to unify in a greater way, as it keeps us from living
different and separate lives. We have to consider one another's schedule, but
riding together allows us to spend more time talking. We have never felt closer
than we do now.

2. **Speak positively about your spouse to others.** Too often,
while with friends or in other group settings, couples take liberty
to jab at one another, pointing out each other's weaknesses and
laughing at them. When you hurt your partner, you hurt yourself. Speaking positively about your spouse's virtues keeps him or
her in the forefront of your own thinking.

When I am a guest speaker at a church where Larry has already spoken,
people get excited to meet me because of the edifying things that Larry has
already said about me. They are ready to learn from me because of his validation. This kind of affirmation causes me to always improve, not wanting to
disappoint anyone, especially him.

3. **Choose your confidants carefully.** Unity will protect the
vulnerabilities in your relationship. On your eight-lane highway
that you enjoy together, you will encounter construction zones
along the way. These improve the pleasure and safety of the
highway and prepare it to meet the new demands of traffic in
the future. The highway does require adjustments and repairs in
order to remain in unity. Different circumstances in life change
the flow of traffic, and we often do not like the hindrances and
intrusions of these unexpected orange barrels. When you find

it difficult to navigate through this construction zone and need some "road-side assistance," choose carefully whom you talk to.

One thing I know for sure is that you do not talk negatively about your spouse to your parents. God will give you the grace to forgive, overlook, and rebuild. However, your family will not have that same grace. They will tend to view your spouse through your negative report long after you have reconciled. Also, when your spouse learns that you have talked about your relational challenges and openly exposed his or her shortcomings, he or she will feel that you have been disloyal. Disloyalty divides unity.

4. **Seek wise counsel.** The road to unity can have rough spots, potholes, swerves and curves. We can work out some issues in our relationships with time, experience, patience and love. However, don't try to navigate your journey alone. If you seem to come to an impasse, a fork in the road, and you don't know which way to turn, get help. Together, please seek wise counsel.

Talking to a mediator or getting personal coaching is a sign of strength, and it indicates that you value unity in your marriage. I recently met a newly married husband and wife who each grew up in a very dysfunctional family. Wisely, after one year of marriage, they chose to add regular counseling to their budget. They wanted to be proactive in assuring that their relationship would have a strong foundation. Together, they submitted to listen and learn, to be corrected and directed. They made unity a high priority.

5. **Pray.** I believe the old adage, "A family that prays together stays together." Never underestimate the power of prayer. Make prayer for your spouse a daily duty because only God can change a human heart. When you realize this, you will stop trying to change your mate and allow God to be God in your life and in theirs. It is amazing how God will answer your prayers; through prayer, He changes both of you!

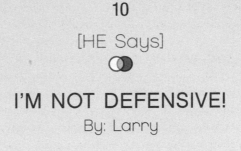

10

[HE Says]

I'M NOT DEFENSIVE!

By: Larry

DEVI SAYS THAT defensiveness is the number one enemy of intimacy in a marriage. Do you know my response to that? "It isn't either. There are other causes; I just can't think of them at the moment." When she tells me that I'm overly sensitive or defensive about something, I respond by saying, "No, I'm not." And when she starts getting even close to suggesting that I have a problem, I immediately begin scanning my mental radar to find someone else to blame. It's critical that I find someone else who is the problem, other than me.

You've probably guessed by now that one of us in this marriage relationship is extremely defensive. Can you guess which one that might be? If you accuse me of being the one, I will deny it. After all, I'm a man. I don't make mistakes, I don't need to apologize, and I'm never, ever wrong. If you think I'm wrong, then that proves who's wrong--you.

Defensive people do not want to inspect themselves to find clues for their failures. Defensive people remain extremely un-teachable because they're never the problem; it's always someone else's fault. Defensive people are very closed, unwilling for people to really get to know them. As Devi says, they always have a defensive, Plexiglas shield in front of them deflecting any attempts others make to try and get to know them. They usually fear getting hurt. Defensiveness truly is the number one enemy to intimacy.

Defensive people do not want to face facts; they will not open themselves up to correction, and they always look for someone else to blame. Defensive people are paranoid about being exposed in a weakness, mistake or perceived failure. Excuses become the cover-up for their failure. They view others as the true culprits and blame circumstances to deflect their own guilt. "I would have been on time, but the traffic was bad." "I would have gotten your car back on time, but my wife was sick." "I would have, but..." becomes the opening statement for every excuse.

When someone asks you why you are late, wouldn't it be refreshing to say, "Because I didn't calculate in advance how bad the traffic would be," or "I simply tried to force too many projects into my allotted time before I left?" Best of all, you could say, "Because I'm an inveterate procrastinator, and I have no one to blame but myself."

Why do we try to blame others instead of taking responsibility for dumb decisions we make, things that don't go right, and messes we create? What's so hard about raising your hand and saying, "It's me; I did it. I'm the problem." I don't think there's a politician in Washington that is capable of saying, "I'm the problem. It's me. Don't blame anyone else because I'm the culprit. Tell me what I need to do to correct it." If there is, I think we should elect him President.

Former President Harry Truman had a plaque on his desk that read, "The buck stops here." That's a great motto for a man who was the only President to use a Nuclear weapon. He assumed total responsibility for his actions, using neither excuses nor blame shifting to escape public criticism. If Republicans didn't exist, Democrats would have no one to blame for the mess the country is in. If Democrats didn't exist, Republicans would have no one to censure and assign guilt to when making their political ads.

Fortunately for Presidents, they can always blame their predecessors. A Vice-President can always hold the President responsible for why he doesn't succeed. Generals can blame their subordinates, and subordinates can blame their generals.

For men, we can always point the finger of guilt at our wives, as Adam did with the defensive blast, "It's that woman you gave me!" And wives have the greatest scapegoat imaginable--the devil. Christians actually love the devil because they can blame him for everything, including things that he didn't actually do.

In my years of working with inmates in prisons, I have rarely found an inmate who will say, "It's me. I was the problem. I have no one else to blame but myself." It's always their mom, dad, girlfriend, the police, the dog, the cat, the teacher, the boss-- anyone but themselves.

I am convinced that a man can never become truly great and still remain defensive. It is the curse of insecure men to never own up to their own issues. Because you're the only one who can fix your mess, unless you own the mess as yours, you will never be able to fix it.

What are some of the signs of a defensive person?

+ You're afraid to own up to a mistake.
+ At the first sign of accusation, you begin looking for someone else to blame.
+ You don't tell the whole truth, but only the part that makes you look good.
+ You're unwilling to listen to the suggestions of others.
+ You're un-teachable; you're unwilling to learn; you know more than others.
+ If someone challenges you, you immediately put that person down.
+ It's hard to admit when you're wrong.
+ It's hard for you to apologize and ask for forgiveness.
+ You don't want to look "less than perfect."
+ It's hard for you to compliment others.
+ You're controlling.
+ You're not open or vulnerable.
+ Your friends don't feel comfortable confronting you.
+ You avoid confrontation.
+ You hide things.

If you could put a check mark beside five or more of these points, there's a strong possibility that YOU'RE A DEFENSIVE CONTROL FREAK! No, let me soften that. You're like the rest of us defensive male animals, always looking for someone else to blame, but inwardly wanting to "man up" to your issues.

WHAT CAN YOU DO?

+ Embrace suggestions.
+ Don't look for scapegoats when you get cornered.
+ Assume blame when something fails and it's your fault.
+ Be painfully honest when you're exposed.
+ Don't hide, like Adam, when you sense the Holy Spirit convicting you.
+ Embrace criticism and see if there is any part of it that you can extract and learn from.
+ Don't fear failure; it's a friend, not an enemy.

- ◆ View mistakes as normal to humanity and not a sin against God.
- ◆ Don't fear being hurt. If you embrace the truth, it will set you free, not hurt you.

Several years ago, I called a Board meeting at our church that included both elders and deacons. When all the men had sat down around the u-shaped table, I asked them one of the most foolish questions I've ever asked. "Is there anything about my leadership that you don't like?" I knew I would get a few negative responses. I had no idea that I would get *twenty* negative responses. While most of them were minor, one man decided to unload all his venom on me. "You listen to no one. If someone tries to correct you, you turn it back on that person. You're totally un-teachable. You're unwilling to listen to any suggestion that anyone else has to say. Things are never your fault." It actually included more than that, but you get the idea.

I was stunned, shocked, embarrassed, hurt, and mad, all at the same time. I quickly closed the meeting, went home, and cried the rest of the night.

The following day, I headed to the Conference Center where I planned to inform the leadership that I would be unable to fulfill my prior commitment to speak for them that day. I didn't need to share the fact that I cried all night, was emotionally drained, felt like a failure, and had nothing to share. I was just going to say I couldn't speak for them. I heard someone once say that they had a friend who had cut them down so deeply they could sit on a paper dollar and dangle their legs. That's how I felt, but I probably would have had room to spare before my feet touched the ground.

But, while driving to the Conference Center, I passed by the exit to my church and automatically pulled off as if to go to my office. I was shocked. It was like someone was turning the wheel of my car to go to my office. In the five right-hand turns that it took to pull into the parking lot of my church, I clearly heard the voice of the Lord speak to me. "Larry, I have tried to tell you that you are defensive by sending you friends, enemies, staff, and your wife, but you've listened to no one. If you do not repent, I will remove the lamp stand from your life."

I instantly knew what the Lord was talking about. I had studied the Book of Revelation enough to know that the lamp stands, or candle sticks, that Jesus walked among in Revelation 2 and 3, described the Churches of Asia Minor. But in my previous study, I had also concluded that the lamp stands were really indicative of the anointing of the Holy Spirit in the Churches. My interpretation was that if I did not repent, Jesus would remove the anointing from my ministry. He didn't mean that I would lose my salvation, but that my ministry would no longer carry that critical, empowering element of the Holy Spirit that insured effectiveness.

I parked my car, walked into my office, and went immediately into the office of the man who had dealt the death-blow. I thanked him for rebuking me. I told him I appreciated the fact that he exposed this defensive issue in my life. I also complimented him for speaking the truth to me in love and not fearing retaliation on my part. At the end of my confession, I was a different man.

I hopped into my car and continued on to the Conference, delivering a powerful and prophetic message to the crowd. Had I not embraced my issues and confessed the sin of my defensiveness, I am convinced there would have been no anointing on that meeting or any that have subsequently followed.

I wish I could say that from that day to this I have never been defensive. That would be a lie. But what is the truth is that defensiveness may pop up on occasion, but it is dealt with and not allowed to dominate. I can willingly embrace the truth no matter how painful it might be, knowing that the truth will always set me free. That's what Jesus said and He was right (see John 8:32).

What happens if someone speaks the truth and it's not in love? Well, I'm still obligated to embrace it. The attitude of someone else can't stop me from being changed, nor is it an excuse for why I shouldn't accept it.

Jamie Buckingham had a great quip. He says that the truth will set you free, but first it will hurt. I agree, but it's a good hurt.

So, babe, tell me the truth. I'll take it like a man, after I've first made ten excuses. No, no, I'm down to one these days.

10

[SHE Says]

I'M NOT DEFENSIVE!
By: Devi

I F TIME COULD promise intimacy in a marriage, it would be a great thing. However, it does not. The number of divorces filed per year of couples married more than twenty years is alarming. Divorce rates among couples over 50 have doubled in the last 20 years, according to a study by Bowling Green State University. In 1990, fewer than one in 10 people who divorced were 50 or older. In 2009, that figure was one in four.

It is entirely possible to navigate through differences and live harmonious with one another and never really be intimate. It is possible to have great sex, hilarious laughter, and peaceful companionship without feeling intimate with one another. When a husband or wife lives with an emotional guard on their heart, they create an emotional wall that the other cannot penetrate. Worse yet is when both husband and wife are defensive. In their relationship, they can grow closer, but defensiveness will prevent them from getting in—being intimate with their hearts. Allowing another person into your heart is to fully trust them with all of your thoughts, good and bad, all of your "secrets," which means you no longer live in secret, and with all of your fears. Intimacy also shares without fearing ridicule, hopes, dreams, and visions, no matter how ridiculous and far-reaching they may seem. Two becoming one is not just a marriage vow repeated at the altar; it is an amazing mystery of the human heart.

TWO BECOMING ONE

True intimacy is two hearts becoming one heart. I have given Larry total authority over my heart and he has given me authority over his heart. There is nothing that Larry can say to me about me that I will not listen to—even when I think he is wrong. I am aware that I have a blind side to myself that I cannot see. If he points out something that needs correction, who am I to not trust that he has my best in mind? His correction is always in love and if I embrace his input in my life, I am the benefactor of personal growth and intimacy with him. You may think, "But my husband corrects me in anger, not love." When that happens, you can still hear what he has to say, sift it, take the good and throw away the bad. Don't let his anger prevent you from receiving correction if you are wrong. His anger is not your problem- it is his. Allowing another person to speak to issues in your character always draws your relationship closer.

A Closer Look

"Let us lay aside every weight, and sin which clings so closely and let us run with endurance the race that is set before us, looking to Jesus, the founder and perfecter of our faith, who for the joy that was set before him endured the cross, despising the shame, and is seated at the right hand of the throne of God." Hebrews 12:1-2

Defensiveness is a weight or an encumbrance that clings closely to your soul. The scripture says that you are to *"lay it aside..."* The dictionary describes defensiveness this way: It is an argument made before a court (an accuser); devoted to preventing or resisting aggression; an argument to justify. Leaders (those who are accustomed to having authority) who display defensiveness are really good at arguing their case to prove their point, justifying their behavior, and protecting themselves. They also excel at telling another person what to do and why. So how does one "lay it aside"?

1. **Face your need to be right** and allow your husband to be right, or at least think he is right. It is really good for his ego. If he is wrong (and you know it), he will not need you to tell him. He will discover it on his own.

2. **Present your case at a different time than he is presenting his case.** This will prevent an argument.

3. **Improve your communication habits.** When you answer with the words "I know", you immediately shut down the other person's input. It is no fun to communicate with someone who already knows everything.

A guest at my Mentoring Mansion's Home Experience Intensive explained the challenges that she and her husband had in their relationship. She worked as a court-room defense attorney and he was a professor of Psychology. Often, he would say to her, "Don't cross examine me." And she would say to him, "Don't psychoanalyze me." I had to laugh. I could easily see how this could play out in their relationship. Although you may not be married to a psychologist or a defense attorney, it is easy to see how we can use the tools of our trade against our spouse when we want to win. If you are a teacher, you could always be teaching your husband. If he is a doctor, he could be diagnosing you and so on.

Stop and think about this: why would you ever want to create a scenario to set up the one you love to lose—especially with you? Most of the time, when we are having "intense fellowship" (fighting or arguing), we do not understand what is really happening between us. Two are trying to become one. It's not easy, but it is possible. Keep trying to drop your guard to "let him in."

UNDERSTANDING DEFENSIVENESS

There are five common causes of defensiveness:

1. Rejection

2. Disappointment

3. Betrayal

4. Embarrassment

5. Failure

Understanding the five causes of defensiveness will help you climb over your husband's defensive wall to get into his heart. You will also realize why you are defensive and will have the courage to take down your own wall, fear by fear, to allow him into your heart. It is important to know that you can never take down another person's defensive emotional wall. Bulldozers do not work. If you try this method, you will be met with a firing squad, become injured and withdraw. However, love can penetrate anything, no matter how immovable the wall seems.

Defensiveness will cause a person to act out of their weakness and not their strength. That reaction is usually to avoid something that is perceived to be personally painful. This pain has roots from one or more of the previously stated five common causes of defensiveness.

Larry came home from a board meeting of our growing church. I had developed a city-wide outreach to women and had recently hosted a ministry event filling the city's convention center. We were filled with vision and our congregation loved and supported us. New land was purchased for expansion, qualified staff hired and fruitful ministry was impacting our city.

> Defensiveness will cause a person to act out of their weakness and not their strength.

With a sober face, Larry told me, "I resigned tonight." I felt like I was on a carnival ride, spinning in a cage that I could not escape and the bottom dropped out. "Why? What happened?" I asked. Larry's defensive reaction in a board meeting resulted in a hurtful loss for our family. His resignation was not because of this meeting directly. He reacted out of his weakness, perceiving and fearing repeat of pain that he had experienced four years earlier.

Often, your spouse's defensive actions are unrelated to your current issue, but are attached to their past. Understanding this will help you navigate your relationship. I stayed very angry with Larry for a few days, then God spoke to me, "You have to allow Larry to be wrong. It's OK with me, so it has to be OK with you. You have plenty of your own turns of being wrong, too." It was then that I could turn loose of my anger (defensiveness) and move forward with the new adventure for our family that his "wrong" created. I clung to Romans 8:28. It is a scripture that we all know, but few of us want to have to live it out!

*And we know that for those who love God **all things work together for good**, for those who are called according to His purpose. Romans 8:28*

Understanding and trusting this truth should remove fear from being wrong. With our best efforts, neither Larry nor I will always be right. Neither will you.

The harsh reality of life is that what happens to us today can affect how we respond to tomorrow unless we take the defensive bull by the horns and bring it to the ground. We do this by embracing what happens to us today and getting the most from it. You are the only one that can take down your wall.

IDENTIFY YOUR REACTIONS

Love bears all things, believes all things, hopes all things, endures all things. Love never ends. 1 Corinthians 13:7-8a

Removing your wall of defensiveness to allow your love to penetrate the heart of your husband is a deliberate decision. Remember, when you put up an emotional wall to keep hurt out, you will also keep love out. I will give you a few common reactions and see if you identify with any of them. Admitting that you react in one of these ways can be your first step to dropping your guard.

1. **I fear rejection.** The fear of rejection will cause a person to harden their heart and attack before being attacked. They will fight back with anger. Anger always pushes back your lover who wants the best for you and is trying to come to you.

2. **I am cynical and sarcastic.** Cynicism and sarcasm is a seemingly acceptable way to put others down. This is often done with humor. But the truth is tearing down your spouse and pointing out their flaws keeps them bound to your own pretense— pretending that you have no flaws of your own.

3. **I blame others.** If you have to explain why you said what you said or did what you did, you are defending your actions and blaming circumstances or people for your behavior. This will prevent you from receiving instruction or correction that could have been a blessing to you.

4. **I act independently.** If you act independently and do not seek wise council or inquire of others, you probably fear you will be judged in the same way you judge others—harshly. In your mind, if you ask to be taught by another, especially your husband, to you, it is an admission that you do not know everything and a threat to their self-perceived image.

Defensiveness is a self-inflicted emotional prison. Your lock is on the inside of your heart and only you hold the keys.

TEAR DOWN YOUR WALL—UNLOCK YOUR DOOR

Self- righteous prophetess...

Early in our marriage and ministry, Larry and I experienced amazing Kingdom impact and success in monumental proportions. God chose to anoint and bless our passionate blind faith. After twelve years, it was our turn to embrace a trial in equal proportions to our success. What we encountered head-on could have been devastating and destructive to our lives, marriage and ministry callings. It was then that we decided that finishing well was more important than beginning well.

> Defensiveness is a self-inflicted emotional prison. Your lock is on the inside of your heart and only you hold the keys.

Over time, having buckled with the pain of failure, Larry and I joined forces and embraced what was "done to us". Rather than blaming others and justifying ourselves, we assumed all of the fault. We accepted that God was the hand behind the hand that hurt us. Larry tore down his defensive wall stone by stone, experience by experience. I allowed him the freedom to be wrong without pointing a finger.

My mother has a plethora of wise-bites that shaped my character. Two of my favorites include: "What's so bad about being wrong?" The fear of failure or the fear of being wrong keeps a defensive person from trying. Life is full of ups and downs, rights and wrongs, triumphs and failures—no one escapes then. The beat of the drum is in the down stroke, the tone of the piano keys reverberate with the down stroke. Our darkest moments have become our greatest victories. To not try is to not achieve. To try is to take the risk to fail or accomplish. Both are victories. It is really not so bad to be wrong, if you admit it. And if you are blamed for being wrong when you are not, remember, it's not so bad to be wrong, when you know that you are not. Either way, you win.

Mother's other wise-bite is her add-on to an old adage: "Don't cry over spilled milk. Just clean it up," Mom would say. If you have been wrong, make the best out of it, take responsibility and move on. It was definitely this kind of training and example that gave me the confidence to embrace my faults, be teachable, and be supportive of others who did not have this kind of emotional support.

LIVING WITH A DEFENSIVE PERSON

It is important to understand how to approach a person who has their guard up and is afraid to trust you with their whole heart. Following are a few guidelines:

1. **Adjust your communication style.** You are not your spouse's teacher. Insecurity and low self-esteem is usually the root cause of their defensiveness nature. Use lots of questions when you communicate with them. Make suggestions rather than give directions. Avoid accusatory talk. "Why did you?" "You should have," "You could have," and "you did." Affirm them. Let them know how important their opinion is to you. Do not push their buttons. Be respectful in your approach. You do not have to walk on eggshells, but graciousness always uses diplomacy. This is love. The worst thing you can say to a defensive person during a conversation is, "You are being defensive." Or worst yet, "Don't be defensive." This will create a pushback every time; you will get either aggression or withdrawal.

2. **Build their Self Esteem.** Support your spouse. Embrace the things they love. Agree with them. Use eye contact when they are talking to you. Affirm their ideas with a nod or a smile. Contribute to their conversation with a question of interest or support. Avoid making comments that challenge what they have said.

3. **Confront with a Surrendered Heart.** If you have a different opinion than your spouse on a serious issue that you believe could be destructive to you or your family, use what I call the "Esther principle." When Esther needed to confront the decision of her husband, she prayed for three days and then entered his presence with a fully surrendered heart. She opened her dialogue with this phrase, *"If it pleases the king..."* She invited her King to a banquet that she prepared and began explaining the problem. She was careful and deliberate. She did not unload on him, threaten him, attack him, but quite the opposite; she surrendered her heart and was willing to take the risk to change

his mind or to live with the consequences of his decision. This is true submission.

DEFENSIVE WOMEN

Defensive women and defensive men behave somewhat differently, although the root causes of defensiveness are the same. Larry addressed men very poignantly so now it is my turn to address women. In the beginning of time, Eve demonstrated two vulnerabilities of women. First, she sought spirituality, "...*to be like God.*" Secondly, she blamed the serpent. "...*the serpent deceived me and I ate.*" Genesis 3

Super spirituality among women becomes an impenetrable wall of defense. They always have the "Word of the Lord" and will not listen to others. Soon, they become superior to their husbands, their pastors, and as one woman said, "God has made me the 'watch man on the wall' to ensure that this church is not in error!" Eve probably wanted to be like God so she could tell Adam what to do! It is precisely this attitude that sets defensive women up to be deceived.

Eve entered into a conversation with a voice that contradicted the Word of God. She reasoned with ideas that were in direct conflict with what God had told Adam. Apparently, she did not fully trust Adam that he heard from God and was not willing to fully submit and embrace the Word of the Lord. When the deceiver approached her, questioning what God actually said, the first mistake she made was to engage in conversation with a thought or idea that is in direct conflict with the Word of God. Eve was not teachable and did not trust that Adam heard from God. Satan misquoted God and misinterpreted what God meant. Satan told Eve, "*Surely you will not die.*" Eve listened and then questioned herself, not trusting what Adam believed. She engaged in a rationalizing conversation that led her to deception. Then she reasoned, "...*the tree was good for food,*" Eve was being practical; and "...*it was a delight to the eyes*", she loved beauty; and the tree would "...*make one wise*" (quotes are from Genesis 3). What could be so wrong with practicality, beauty and wisdom? Let's go for it! Adam, look what we can accomplish. Sensibility, beauty, and intelligence...that's what women want. But was that what God wanted? When God approached them, Adam and Eve defensively "hid themselves." They didn't want to face what they had done. Adam's defense was hiding and blaming his wife; Eve's defense was hiding and blaming the devil. "*Adam was not deceived but the woman was deceived and became a transgressor.*" 1 Timothy 2:14. Adam disobeyed God and did not assume the responsibility for his disobedience. He knew the Word of the Lord, but did not fear the Lord and was led astray by

115

his vulnerability to the woman he loved. He listened to her and did not protect her by refusing to compromise. Eve was deceived by Satan. These are two very different things. Disobedience and deception led this couple to an outcome of harsh difficulty and loss, creating pain for the innocent generations to follow.

Blaming is the other characteristic that women use as their defensive weapon. And "super spiritual women" will always blame the devil. "Satan is attacking our marriage." No, it's not Satan, it's you not respecting and trusting your husband's wisdom.

> *Wives, be subject to your own husbands, so that even if some do not obey the word, they may be won without a word by the conduct of their wives, when they see your respectful and pure conduct." I Peter 3:1-2 "... adorn the hidden person of the heart with the imperishable beauty of a gentle and quiet spirit, which in God's sight is very precious." v.4*

Surrendering your defensiveness and uniting in trust to your husband's ability to hear from God will protect you from error. Defensive women tend to become unteachable, uncorrectable, sarcastic, and blaming. All men will disengage from this behavior and shut down. Most men will give you your way and you will not like where your way will take you. Take down your defensive wall by giving others permission to teach you what you do not know, by correcting your wrong rude behavior, and by assuming responsibility for your relational tensions. Edify others without looking for personal approval. Remove from your vocabulary the "I know" response. As soon as someone else tells you something, rather than saying, "I know" which causes that person to stop, replace "I know" with "Really?" "Okay," "Tell me more"...etc. This new response will open your heart for input. You will love the awesome input that others will give you. The saddest thing about living with a defensive wall is that not only does your defense keep out hurt, but the wall on your heart will also keep out love.

> Edify others without looking for personal approval.

Drop you guard and embrace the blessings that are waiting for you through the awesome people that God has put into your life.

11

CAUTION ZONES—WATCH FOR RED FLAGS

By: Larry

ED FLAGS ARE typically those red warning signs that are held or posted by construction workers indicating the need for extreme caution. People who ignore such warnings do so at their own peril. Marriage also has red flags that are scriptural sign-posts to warn you of likely danger or, if unheeded, probable disaster.

This chapter on Red Flags is intended to warn you of potential danger in the lives of leaders who live together. Though this list is not exhaustive, it is at least an attempt to ward off some of the most obvious dangers that we have seen leaders succumb to over the past fifty years of ministry. If you heed the red flags, you will save your marriage, your family and your future. If you ignore them, you can forfeit everything. What begins as flirting with adventure ends with courting disaster.

There is no person who is so spiritual as to be immune from these potential disasters. As Paul said, *"I discipline my body and keep it under control, lest after preaching to others I myself should be disqualified."* I Corinthians 9:27. It's not that Paul is threatening eternal damnation. He is saying that if we don't discipline our fleshly appetites, God won't use us. We will be shelved, disqualified. Do you think that God will use an undisciplined person who continually chooses to ignore His warning signs? It will never happen.

Below I've listed some of the red flags that I've encountered.

DIVORCE DISCUSSIONS

Divorce has now been made easy in our courts; therefore, it has become common in our society. Now, couples banter around the word "divorce" using it as a threat on a regular basis to keep their spouse in line. I can't imagine

117

anything unhealthier. *Divorce* is not a word in my household dictionary. Devi and I won't consider it; it's not in our vocabulary. We don't speak of it, and we don't like others to even mention it. In an interview, Ruth Graham was asked, "Have you ever considered divorce?" Ruth Graham wittingly said that divorcing her husband, Billy, was never an option, but she had considered murder. Of course, this statement was made in jest. That was a cute way to reinforce her convictions that divorce was not an option in their marriage, even when they faced tough times.

I'm so unbending in my convictions that I don't like any jokes that relate to divorce or anyone who speaks about marriage in a pejorative or levities manner. Marriage is to be held in high regard.

It wasn't too many decades ago that few people in the United States or Western culture even considered divorce. Back then, if you got married, you stayed married, at any cost. Now, often divorce is considered an option even before the marriage ceremony. "Well, if things don't work out, I can always get a divorce." It's even written into pre-nuptial agreements. And Hollywood doesn't help any with its shallow approach to marriage both in movies and in real-life. Tabloid magazines must get ecstatic when hearing of another pending divorce among celebrities. It's great grist for gossip mongers. They rarely rejoice over marriages that have experienced fidelity and longevity. I guess it doesn't sell many magazines. Although divorce is socially accepted, there remains an inner sadness when someone's marriage fails, regardless if it is a politician, an entertainer, a preacher, or a family member.

Please understand that you cannot continually bring up the topic of divorce in your conversations without it opening up the possibility of divorce actually occurring. When you said your marriage vows, you should have slammed the doors of even thinking about divorce, let alone doing it. What greater legacy could you leave your children than for them to see your commitment to marriage? It will give them character to not quit when life gets tough. They can embrace, "...for better or for worse, until death do us part," because you did.

The Bible is clear that "God hates divorce." I hate it, too.

Recently, a man was telling me that his wife was threatening divorce. He boasted that he told her his commitment to their children would be as such that they would be OK. When I reported his statement to Devi, she went ballistic. "No, the kids will not be alright," then listed a litany of reasons why that is absolutely false. Kids are never all right when the mother and father, whom they love so deeply, no longer demonstrate that same kind of love to each other. Those of us who counsel couples on a regular basis have to deal with the negative consequences of divorce. You have no idea the damage that it causes to children that decades of counseling cannot eradicate. Children, with broken hearts because their parents are not together become adults with broken hearts who seldom live in committed, long-term, loving relationships. They fear the pain of separation because they have already lived through it once in their lifetime. Are children a good reason to stay married? Absolutely. You can rekindle your flame later, if needed, but give "later" a chance. The greatest gift you can give to your children is a mother and father who live together.

Years ago, when divorce was not as common as it is now, a lady came to me confessing that she was going to divorce her husband. I immediately asked her why. She was very candid. "It's very simple; I don't love him anymore." When I suggested to her that, "I don't love him anymore," was not a biblical reason to divorce, she countered with, "I don't care." Now that's a problem when "I don't care" overrides the biblical injunction against divorce. Where is the fear of God? Where is the fear of negative consequences to our decisions? For you, your spouse, and your children.

The interesting thing is that she never once considered that she was setting herself up for failure, for sin, for a dysfunctional family and for misery. I have no idea how many spouses I have talked to who regretted their decision to divorce. Enough, I assure you, to confirm the fact that the grass is not always greener on the other side. In fact, it's often dry and dead.

I am not condemning anyone who has been divorced. I am suggesting that you consider the possibility of divorce as not only a Red Flag, but also a Red Banner, a Red Billboard, a Red Blimp and anything else that is red, including blood. It's deadly. Our culture, society, and families are all being systematically destroyed by this massive problem. We should have taken care of it when it was a Red Flag before it became a Red Army, and marched in to destroy our families.

It's quite possible that a spouse or couple desiring to get a divorce will at some time approach you as a leader. Please don't be guilty of encouraging it. Unless there is physical abuse or ongoing extra-marital affairs, do everything in your power to keep it from happening. When you stand before God, you'll be glad that you resisted it, in your own marriage and others as well.

Years ago, my daughter faced the uncertain and fearful specter of a broken marriage through spousal infidelity and an unwanted divorce. I have never seen anyone more tenacious. She retained love and respect for her husband, steadfastly resisted divorce and within months, saw her husband's complete repentance and restoration. Divorce was not an option. Prayer prevailed and love overcame every negative emotion, including the monster of bitterness. I'm immensely proud of both my daughter and son-in-law. I'd like to make a bronze statue of both of them and write on it a caption: "Divorce—you lost."

If all things are possible with God, then surely healing a marriage is one of them. If prayer can move mountains, then start interceding. If love covers a multitude of sins, then release the floodgates of love. But don't agree with that demonic spirit of divorce that refuses to deal with the underlying issues and seeks shallow, temporary solutions.

NO OTHER WOMAN

This is my conviction and this is my life-style. There is no other woman in the world, as far as I am concerned, other than my wife. No one deserves my attention, my affection, my emotional commitment, my visual fixation, or my heart than my wife. No woman is too pretty, intelligent, creative or vivacious to allure me. If you're romantically interested in me, then you're wasting your time. I'm not interested in you, period. I won't text you, talk on the phone with you, FaceBook you, take you home after work, Tweet you, meet you at the water cooler or after hours.

Years ago, Devi informed me that she spotted a woman in our church who would deliberately wait for me to finish greeting people after service so that she could give me a "pastoral" hug. At first, I thought Devi was being overly sensitive. Not so. She was absolutely right. Sometimes, it takes a woman to know the intention of another woman. Maybe that's true of men as well. He can spot another man who is on the prowl. She called it correctly and I had not even noticed. Listen to your spouse.

This was not some innocuous hug, but a calculated physical gesture by a seductive woman. I am so glad that Devi was able to turn my blinded eyes into the reality of a seductive embrace that could have destroyed my life, marriage and ministry. Devi held up the red flag for me and I took heed, though at the time, it looked more pink than red. I just couldn't see it. To this day, I am overly cautious about women who are too friendly. The closer a woman gets, the farther I move away from her. The only woman that has entrance into my life is Devi. Forward women cause me to retreat, and they don't even have to be wearing red for me to put my car in reverse.

Ladies, it is the same for you. No other man should have your heart. Sharing feelings and intimate confidences is a no trespassing zone. If you find yourself dressing in a way that will attract the attention of someone other than your spouse, change clothing. It is common for leaders, men and women, to work in close association with other men and women. Smart women like smart men. Be careful when you synergize intellectually with another man. This can become an expected attraction. Avoid business lunches alone with another man and always drive your own car rather than riding with another man. Also, keep your hands to yourself. Outgoing personalities are common to leader-women. Small gestures of touching can create inappropriate signals to others who may not live by your standards. These are common-sense guidelines to avoid unnecessary temptations.

SECRETS: "SHHH, DON'T TELL."

The devil loves secrets and dark places. God loves truth and light. If we love, serve and follow God, we must be people of openness, hiding nothing.

And no creature is hidden from his sight, but all are naked and exposed to the eyes of him to whom we must give account. Hebrews 4:13.

Jesus said that *"nothing is covered that will not be revealed, or hidden that will not be known."* Matthew 10:26. Jesus then amplifies His statement in Luke 12:3 when He declares, *"Therefore whatever you have said in the dark shall be heard in the light, and what you have whispered in private rooms shall be proclaimed on the housetops."* A quick review of the recent expose' of several politicians and preachers is sufficient to let you know that whatever is done in secret can easily be picked up by social media, ensuring that your private indiscretion will soon become public disgrace. Secrets have a habit of destroying the best of reputations and leaders.

In the Garden of Eden, Adam's fall resulted in man's first attempt to hide things from God. When God asked Adam, *"Where are you?"*, Genesis 3:9, it wasn't because He didn't know. God wanted Adam to recognize that nothing is hidden from Him. From then until now, mankind has attempted to keep things not only from God, but also from each other. We have become master tailors and seamstresses, excelling in sewing fig leaves together to cover up our sin. If you hide things from your spouse, you know that sin is soon to follow.

Secrets are major **Red Flags**. If there is something I cannot tell my spouse, you can count on it not being from God. If I can't tell my spouse what I'm thinking, something is wrong. If I can't tell my spouse what I've been watching, something is wrong. If I don't want to tell my spouse the cost of something I purchased, I have a problem. If I can't tell my spouse the real reason I'm staying late at work, my secret has opened the door for the devil to walk in. If I can't tell my spouse who I have been texting, sin is crouching at the door. Secrets and sins are bedfellows.

If you can't tell your spouse, it's not of God. You can tell your spouse everything. In a healthy marriage, there are no secrets.

UNDERMINING EACH OTHER'S AUTHORITY

As a child growing up, I would hear my oldest brother's wife say to their kids, "Oh, you don't have to listen to your dad. He doesn't know what he's talking about anyway." Sometimes, she would say it in a pejorative way and at other times, it would be comedic, like, he's such a dunce. But whether it was framed as a slam against him or in a semi-joking way, it was always undermining. Their family was torn apart by her systematic put-down of my brother until it ended in her divorcing him and the kids disrespecting him. She began believing her own lies. Even as a child, I would cringe at her conniving, manipulating ways to make herself look superior and him inferior. Often, she made her negative jabs in jest. Every hurtful thing she said against my brother hurt me. I knew intuitively that it was wrong. My parents did not relate this way and I did not want this in my marriage.

Proverbs says that when you dig a pit for someone to fall into, you fall into it yourself, and a stone will fall back on the one who starts it rolling. Proverbs 26:27. You cannot undermine your spouse in the eyes of your children or others without it destroying you. The stone of undermining and usurping your spouse's confidence, identity, and/or authority will return to crush you.

I feel so sorry for parents who have chosen to turn their children against their mother or father. They have no idea how destructive their actions are. Everyone loses. They will destroy both their children and themselves in the process. Generations to come will be hurt by their behavior. In order to ensure God's blessings, you must edify your spouse at all times and especially in the presence of your children.

Nothing is more important to maintaining stability and health in a family than a united front. If your wife gives a directive to your children, agree with it, even if you need to discuss it later. "Son, what did your mother tell you to do? Then do it." "What did your dad say? Well, I agree with him."

Don't allow your children to pit you against each other. They begin this game shortly after birth and routinely try it throughout childhood and adolescence. Go ahead and frustrate the daylights out of your children by being in unity with the decision of your spouse.

THE CHIEF DESTROYER—THE "S" FACTOR

Adultery is NOT the chief destroyer of marriage--selfishness is. Lest someone think that I'm minimizing the potential danger of affairs, let me assure you the reason I mentioned it above was to emphasize its deadly impact. There is something far more subtle and fatal, and that is selfishness. In my opinion, selfishness is the one common denominator of all marital difficulties. When leaders live together, it is too tempting to be motivated by your own goals, responsibilities, and life-styles.

After fifty years in ministry, I have never—let me repeat— never had any couple come into my office for counseling where selfishness was not their major issue. Surface issues always arise, such as money, "I don't love him (her) anymore," infidelity, or lack of communication, but all of these causes, inevitably boil down to selfishness.

We can easily identify selfishness by one attitude, which is "Me first." If you were to consider the other person as more important than yourself, as Philippians 2:3 says, selfishness would no longer be an issue. Change your "Me first" attitude to "You first" and you will never find yourself in the office of a marriage counselor. Selfishness will diminish and die over night, if you take such a stance.

Selfishness will destroy any marriage or other relationships, including those within the family, the church, the workplace, or the nation. Selfishness not only opens the door for a host of Red Flags, it also waves a Red Flag for a herd of bulls to come charging at you, destroying everything in their path. Nothing is more destructive than selfishness. The crooner who sang about doing things "My way" didn't know how lethal his philosophy was. Getting or doing things "My way" destroys any possibility of success in life. Plus, it denies the very essence of the Gospel that puts God first, others second and you last. I have a suggestion; let's write a new song entitled, I'll Do It *Your* Way, effectively crippling selfishness, the Number One destroyer of marriages and families. I challenge you to find any root problem that is not centered on selfishness. Even the root of bitterness is grafted in from the root of selfishness. You don't just "get rid" of selfishness; you have to deliberately deny yourself and put your spouse first. *Selflessness* has to replace *selfishness*.

Enjoy your journey together as you esteem one another and navigate your lives carefully through your construction zones.

THE TRAUMA OF TRANSITIONS

Benjamin Franklin said that two things in life remain inevitable: death and taxes.

He's right. And I've got another inevitability that I could add to his list—transition. Changes are inevitable and they always carry the potential for rocking the boat at best or capsizing it at worst. When one leadership partner goes through a transition, it always affects the other. Quite often, the one that is most deeply affected by the change is not the one who makes the decision for change, but rather, it is the one who has to conform to the decision that is made.

It is impossible to experience changes in plans, vision, goals, locations, positions, occupations or staff without an attending emotional trauma. Even when you know that the impending change is God's will, you can still experience trauma. It takes time to adjust. It takes time to sort out the various emotions involved; in addition, you will likely experience pain. Understand, life can be very unsettling at these times.

Transition can carry a variety of consequences. Quite often, it will include separation from friends and family. Sometimes, it will thrust you into a totally new and unfamiliar environment. Occasionally, it will mean an income loss. And you know how insecure that can make you feel. Transition can result from a bad decision that brings negative consequences. At other times, the change can initially look troublesome only to discover later that it was one of the best decisions you have ever made. We can learn a lot in retrospect. "Time will tell" is more than a trite expression. It's a very accurate way of assessing how your past affects your present and future.

Can you imagine how the wives must have felt when the twelve disciples abruptly dropped the news that they would leave their fishing boats and other previous workplaces to follow a total stranger named Jesus from Nazareth? I can just hear their Jewish wives exclaiming, "Oy veh, have you lost your mind?" In hindsight, we can see that they absolutely made the right decision. I think we can correctly assume, however, that their wives didn't see it that way—at least not at first. They only knew that they were losing their husbands, the fathers of their children, and their incomes all at the same time.

Unilateral leadership decisions can put relationships in danger. The non-deciding spouse can feel betrayed, not valued, abandoned and left out of the decision. Early in our marriage, I unilaterally made decisions, leaving my wife out of the loop. I thought I knew what "God" wanted and made a headship decision, forgetting that it should have been a "leaders"-ship decision. That left my wife emotionally drained, as she had to deal with the trauma of transition without having been part of the process. I knew what I was doing and why I was doing it, but I hadn't communicated my thoughts to her. And although I didn't include her in the decision, I expected her to be part of the consequences. We both suffered because of my inconsideration. Communication is absolutely essential during transition times. Talk, talk, talk, talk, and more talk.

Not only do transitions require talk, but also time. Time must pass for one to gain a clear perspective. Even if you make an absolute right decision, you still must build a time lapse into the transition so you can see the whole picture and gain a clear understanding of the outcome. Both of you need time to sort out the details. Understand from the get go that you can't rush transitions.

The same principle applies when a crisis arises and you have to make a transition. For example, the death of a spouse, business partner, or family member brings a need for transition. In these situations, time is always your ally. Watch God use time to heal the wounds of unwanted transitions.

I've never experienced a change in jobs, homes, administrative adjustments, positions, or employees without some form of emotional shock. Even when I knew it was God's will, I still experienced trauma of some sort. The nature of the beast is that change is unsettling, disturbing, and at times, painful. But God-directed change always produces good results, if we just wait for it.

I've cried for weeks when leaving friends and family to follow God to a new location. I've gone through huge times of self-doubt every time I have resigned from a church to pursue another ministry. Changes in staff inevitably disconcert and unnerve me as well. Our flesh loves the security of the familiar. Disturb the status quo and you set yourself up for pain. But change is not only inevitable, it is necessary, and so is the pain of change. God is the only one who does not change. The rest of us must.

Enjoy your journey together as you esteem one another and navigate your lives carefully through your construction zones.

11
[SHE Says]

CAUTION ZONES—WATCH FOR RED FLAGS
By: Devi

WHEN RED FLAGS are displayed, they represent something greater than mere caution, they indicate *change*. Larry describes a construction zone bearing red flags of caution. The reason those flags were placed in a construction zone is because of change. Old roads are repaired and new ones are built. This is not negative, it is positive; however, we must adjust what was common to us in order to embrace the new development. We live in Dallas/Fort Worth, TX metropolis. I'm sure that we are the Mecca of construction zones. Dallas must manufacture red flags—or should I say, "Orange cones"—there seems to be thousands of them.

Everything about a construction zone is inconvenient. It changes the direction that we drive, tries our patience, and fills our car with dirt. Nothing about it is fun during process. The best way to tolerate intrusion is to stay focused on the awesome outcome. This first thing that happens is the sign goes up, "Caution, you have just entered a construction zone." Speed limits are reduced and everything slows down and sometimes even stops. This means things are not going to be the same. Old things are passing away and some things are becoming new. In reconstruction, what is good remains and often improved. What is not-so-good is removed.

When change has taken place in your marriage (and it will), it most likely means you have changed and so has your spouse. Thank GOD we all change! Your interests change, your body changes, and as a leader, perhaps what you are leading has changed.

Navigating change in a construction zone requires focus, attention, and carefulness. So it is in a marriage. Do not be so consumed and distracted that you do not notice that things have changed. It can be like texting while driving.

Distraction may swerve you into the wrong lane and you may miss the detour that will take you to your destination—a loving long-lasting marriage.

So, let's look at what I believe cannot be overlooked.

NOTICE YOUR SPEED

Are you living your life in the fast lane? The sign reads, "SLOW down". The price is always high when you drive too fast in the red-flag zone—double fines. Managing life in today's world is a real challenge. With the advantage and disadvantage of the internet, it is easy to become too overly scheduled, especially when leaders live together. Over scheduling will disconnect you, if you are not careful. It is easy to allow too much time to lapse without meaningful connection.

When I am over scheduled and my calendar controls me rather than me controlling my calendar, my calendar then controls Larry. My commitments change his options. It is the same with his calendar. Sometimes, his new commitments will change my options. The outcome is feeling trapped.

I want to give Larry my attention, spend time with my family, grandchildren and great grandchildren and I want fun-time with friends. But when I have overscheduled my life with projects, which I also love, speaking commitments, publishing deadlines, and the like, guess what happens. You are right! I become filled with anxiety. Then, I also have Larry's time demands to deal with—his calendar, his schedule. When I am anxious, I get aggressive and direct. Unlike me, when Larry is pressed, he becomes emotionally distant—he shuts down. Life in the fast lane for long periods of time can distance and disease healthy relationships.

Together, we demonstrate the two common ways to deal with anxiety: I get busier and Larry takes naps. Neither of these are relational developers; they are relational dividers. Caution! Red Flag.

I remember one time when we experienced a dramatic change. We transitioned from a large church senior pastor in a capital city to planting an inner city church in an economically depressed city. We moved from the city where our married daughter and grandchildren lived. I was speaking more than ever to supplement our income. Larry and I were not talking much by virtue of the situation that we had trapped ourselves in. We were both very busy. We made severe cutbacks in our life-style to afford Larry's new direction in ministry. We sold our second car. The church was five blocks from our home and we rationalized that walking would be good for us. It was very good for us, but in a very different way.

Living with one car caught us by surprise! What we thought would be a difficulty became a blessing. Larry and I had to communicate our schedules, prefer one another, and we had lots of talking time in the car. We connected again. He drove me places and picked me up. I did the same for him. Often, I jokingly say to couples, "If you feel like you have disconnected from your spouse and you no longer have things in common, sell your second car and drive one car for one year. Then see how you feel." What we thought would be a short-term sacrifice has become a life-style. We still have only one car. We like it this way.

It is very important that you take breaks, slow down, and live with margins. A margin is the space on each side of the paper that is blank. This gives you room for adjustments, additions and subtractions. Margins keep you punctual and peaceful. They are like the wide shoulders on the road, the emergency "pull-over" lane. Do not crowd your time, trying to fit one more thing in. Rather, evaluate what things you can eliminate.

A few years ago, I ended my year with internal stress. Everything in my life on the outside looked great—success in my achievements, love in my marriage, and enough money to pay my bills. I asked the Lord, "How can I live my life differently? What adjustments can I make?" I realized that I seldom stopped working. I spent hours per weeks in airplanes and the first thing I would do is get out my computer. I wrote articles, made lists and created more work for everyone who worked for me. I believed that God spoke to me to put my computer away while on the airplane and read, but only read things that I know nothing about. This meant that I could not read my Bible while flying. Previously, I read to study and prepare for my next lecture, sermon, or speech…whatever you want to call it. I am a public speaker. In short, when I read, I was still working.

I was in a rut, and ruts in roads do not make for safe driving. I distinctly remember this was during the competitive Democratic primary race between Barak Obama and Hillary Clinton. So the first books I read were books about Obama and Hillary. This took me on a journey of change—change for the good. Later, I read Allen Greenspan's autobiography; I knew nothing about economics! I read *INFIDEL*; I knew nothing about the tragic lives of Muslim women. Dozens of books later led me to a discovery about myself that I did not know and has been the greatest thing that has happened for me. I read six to eight hours per week in airplanes and learned so much. The red flag slowed me down, changed my pace and I am better informed. This is now my life-long commitment and my internal anxiety to that degree has never returned.

NOTICE CHANGE IN YOUR TALK

The best way to gauge changes in your relationship is to listen to your conversations. Examine the content of your conversations and the frequency of your conversations. Have you stopped talking? Do you feel impatient when your spouse wants to talk about things that are not important to you? Are you laughing together and sharing stories? Do you seek one another's wisdom when you are making decisions in your area of responsibility?

I'm sure you have noticed couples dining in restaurants that sit through an entire meal and never say a word. Larry and I had just placed our order, he excused himself to finish a text before putting away his cell phone and I took out a pen and paper to make of list for the following day. A little time passed and we were aroused from our concentration by the waiter delivering our beverages. We were both pre-occupied and neither of us was talking. I then noticed the couple beside us, at their linen covered table with napkins on their laps, she was reading a book on her Kindle, and he was reading his e-mail on his iPhone while they were both eating their entrees.

I looked across the table at Larry and called his attention to this silver haired couple. I began talking to Larry a bunch of nonsense. I smiled, laughed, flirted, and made him laugh. Here is what I said, "Others are looking at us too, and from this day forward, I will pretend that we are talking and having fun, even if you are not "here" in the moment. We will NOT become one of those!" Then and there, we noticed that we had changed, and not for the better. He laughed at me and said, "Tell me what you want me to say and I'll say it."—so typical of my humorous, non-verbal husband.

Keep yourself interesting and learn about your spouse's interests so you have things in common to talk about. My father loved sports and my mother loved to read. So mother read the sports page in the newspaper every day while Daddy watched the games. He knew all of the stats and names of players and so did Mom. Did she love sports? Not necessarily, but she learned about Daddy's interests so they had common things to talk about. Mother was a Post-Master. Daddy attended all of her business conventions and got acquainted with her peers in the business. They shared in one another's interests.

As you each change and grow, continue to learn about each other and your newfound interests. It will keep you talking.

NOTICE CHANGE IN YOUR TONE

Frequent outbursts of anger toward your spouse is not how you related before you said "I DO." Speaking to one another in harsh tones and loud voices is not what won the affection of your spouse. Neither will it keep their affection. Listen to yourself. Have you changed? Proverbs 15:1 says that a gentle answer will turn away wrath. Anger will always be a viable emotion to express displeasure. It only becomes harmful when it is uncontrolled and aimed at another person. Practice talking to one another in a gentle tone of voice. In our home, I did not allow my children to yell from room to room and I did not yell at them, calling for them to come to me. The rule was, if you want to talk to me, come to where I am. And by the way, I am not deaf. There is no reason to raise your voice.

Larry is a gentle man by nature. I have never heard him raise his voice in anger. He gets mad. His face gets red. He speaks directly, but not loudly. Now me, I can become passionate about what I believe and when I want to make a point, it is easy for me to be loud. I was born loud. Mother said that I cried loudly. When I was a child, Mother would say, "Devi, remember, your voice carries." That was Mother's proverbial positive way of saying, "Don't be so loud."

To keep our "discussions of passion" tame, Larry has been known to say to me, "Devi, don't use that tone of voice." At that moment, I had a choice, to honor his request or to resist it. I made the right choice and heeded the red flag.

Managing this caution zone now will later give you the benefit of navigating your life on a brand newly paved pathway. Remember, you cannot drive on two sides of the road. You are only responsible for your lane. You have no control over your spouse's choices.

NOTICE A CHANGE IN YOUR PRIORITIES

When everyone else and everything else takes priority over your spouse, you are driving in the wrong lane. You can tell me that you value marriage and your spouse is important to you. It is then that I want to say to you, "Then, show me your calendar and your checkbook. And I'll tell you if you are driving in the right lane."

The way you spend your time and your money reveals your true values. If your weekly calendar does not reflect time spent with your spouse, you are not sustaining a good relationship and for sure, you are not growing a great relationship. It does not really matter how you spend your time together; you just need to be together, supporting one another in both of your interests and responsibilities. In our lives, not only do we live together, but we work together. We travel together, minister together, grocery shop together, wash the car together, and clean the yard together. I cook and Larry cleans up my mess, and then we eat together. We really like each other. We live in the priority of one another.

Now, we also both love our times alone. Together, we agree to give each other space. Even when Larry is in another country, he is my priority. I stay connected by praying for him, communicating with him and planning for his homecoming. When Larry comes home, everything shifts. I cook what he likes; I'm home when he is home. We are on a perpetual honeymoon because we have made one another our priority.

Also, look at your checkbook. How much money do you personally spend on your spouse and their personal interests? Are you buying gifts for one another? When you eat in restaurants, do you go where your spouse desires or do you always insist on the least expensive place to eat? Do you eat in lovely restaurants while on business and only go to cheap ones on your date nights? It is one thing to carefully plan a budget and another thing to be miserly when it comes to spending on your husband or wife. Look at your home. Do you prioritize update spending to make your home a place of comfort and pleasure for your spouse? Maybe your husband needs a new comfortable chair and the wife needs an outdoor table for cozy meals together. Perhaps you love to golf and your spouse loves to travel. Plan to spend on both. Ask yourself, "Is our spending lop-sided? Are we investing in our relationship?" Avoid doing things alone because it is cheaper to pay for one rather than two. Compare what you spend on your children's activities and what you spend on your marriage. Your children will be with you only 18 years and your marriage is for a lifetime. Prioritize.

NOTICE CHANGE IN YOUR RESPECTFUL BEHAVIOR

Respect is a feeling of deep admiration for someone or something elicited by their abilities, qualities, or achievements. It is impossible to live in a healthy flourishing relationship in an environment of criticism, judgment, and negativity. Too often, we justify disrespectful behavior based on what someone else has done. The common stresses and changes in life cause all of us to react in unbecoming ways at times. However, I cannot allow someone else's bad choices to determine what kind of person that I want to be.

I'm talking about you taking the responsibility to safely navigate your personal behavior. The crazy way others may behave at times or drive with "road rage" in their construction zones, is not your responsibility. But how you behave, your response to your spouse, especially when their behavior is less than honorable, can make all the difference in the world where your relationship will end up.

Stop blaming your spouse for your uncontrolled reactions to their less-than-sensitive choices. No one else "makes" you do what you do. Conduct yourself in a manner worthy of honor. Chances are, others will follow.

In his letter to the church in Ephesus, Paul encourages husbands to love their wives and the wives to respect their husbands. Love respects and respect loves. One cannot function without the other.

Here is my take from Ephesians 5:33: *Let each one of you love his wife as himself, and let the wife see that she respects her husband.* You would hope that if a person responds to you in love, that respecting them will automatically follow. But that is not always the case. Too often, a man or a woman behaves in disrespectful ways toward their spouse because of their inner pain and turmoil. This uncaring behavior is not based on another person's behavior, but it is a result that is coming from his or her own heart.

Respect is an attitude of a position that you choose to live in regardless of someone else. To be respectful is a choice that you make for yourself. What kind of person do you want to be? One who puts others down, tears them up, or a person who positions yourself to respond with respect, regardless of what is coming at you.

When the verse in Ephesians says, "*. . . and let the wife see that she respects her husband,*" that means it is MY responsibility to respect, regardless if my husband is being disrespectful. This is the choice that I have made. I believe that wives were specifically addressed in this way because it is so easy for us to be emotional and behave in ways that hurt others, especially our husbands. Husbands' egos are so significant in their masculinity that Paul addresses this in his admonition to "*. . . love your wives in the same way you love yourself.*"

Sometimes, the dictionary says it best. In verb form, *respect* has regard for the feelings, wishes, rights, or traditions of others. *Respect* avoids harming or interfering. *Respect* agrees to recognize and abide by requirements. One of the most important attributes in healthy relationships is respect and agreeing to abide by God's requirements.

Larry's red flags and mine are very different, but equally important. We have both drawn from our personal and professional lives. Thousands of couples in pastoral counseling give Larry accurate assessment of common reoccurring issues in marriage. If these red flags are ignored, they can become marriage collisions. Some collisions are repairable and others are not. Unfortunately, the longer a person lives in a dysfunctional relationship, the more difficult it becomes to function in a healthy, loving relationship.

I have addressed directly likely things that happen when leaders live together. Take notice as you navigate through your construction zone changes and, like Larry and me, you will not only have a long-lasting marriage, but you will love living your lives together.

12

[HE Says]
⊙⊙

NO ONE WINS ALONE
By: Larry

I n 1936, King Edward VIII of Great Britain announced that he would be abdicating the throne of the United Kingdom. He was king for less than a year and was never crowned. What he gave up his throne for was to marry the twice-married American socialite, Wallis Simpson. Edward had had relationships with a succession of older married women, but had never married. His decision to marry Mrs. Simpson was only one of many tragic decisions that he made during his life-time.

King Edward's decision to abdicate meant that he would spend the remainder of his life estranged from his family. He refused even to write his mother. He was also required to forfeit his title of "His Holiness," lost nearly all of his honors and had to settle for the humiliating title of Duke of Windsor.

His brother, King George VI, refused to answer his daily phone calls because he knew they would be solicitations for money. Neither was he allowed to return to his homeland until the very end of his life. The plans that he made for his funeral indicated a desire to be buried in Baltimore, MD, but the gracious involvement of the Royal Family after his death acquiesced and allowed him to be buried in England.

Edward spent virtually all of his adult life in other nations, particularly France, though for a short stint, he was Governor of the Bahamas, something he considered quite below his dignity and status in life. Quite often, his actions, such as befriending Hitler, caused the British Crown great embarrassment and anguish.

Could there be anything more tragic? To me, it is heartbreaking. He was born into royalty, raised as a prince, proclaimed crowned King, then lost it all. Though he was a king, he settled for a non-descript, fruitless life estranged from his family, deprived of his inheritance and self-condemned to a life of humiliation. Just reading his biography makes me want to cry.

The easiest way for me to explain and rationalize Edward's behavior is that he just made poor choices. God knows that he left a plethora of examples of poor choices if one needed a proof text, including casting away his glorious inheritance for a twice-married woman. I find myself unwilling, however, to settle for the most immediate and obvious rationale that Edward's life was a result of his poor choices, even though that is the case in part. To me, that's too trite an answer.

Kings are supposed to turn their princes into Kings. Queens are supposed to turn their princesses into queens. Leaders are supposed to raise up leaders. Successful people are supposed to replicate their success in their children. Is there a principle that was missed in Edward's case?

Listen to the words of Edward's father, King George V. "After I am dead," King George V said, "The boy will ruin himself in 12 months." Wow! I hope Edward didn't hear that. "I hope that my oldest son (Edward) will never marry and have children," presciently laying the verbal suggestion of the accession of his youngest son, Prince Albert (King George VI). I hope Edward didn't hear that either. I wonder what else was said either to Edward or other family members about him that caused a prince to act in so many un-princely ways. Why would one with so much potential deliberately ship-wreck his life?

I'm not trying to write off Edward's indiscretions and bad choices as being insignificant as it relates to the reason his life ship-wrecked. I'm just suggesting that if we look deeper into why he made those poor decisions, maybe we can find a more accurate reason behind his failures. Are there principles that we can glean from this tragedy that can allow our marriage and families to succeed in royalty where he failed? After all, those of us who are in Christ are of royal lineage.

Maybe the prince never felt like a prince because others, namely his dad, reminded him of how unqualified he was as a prince. Maybe the prince felt out of place in palaces and stately dinners. Maybe he felt like a failure at college, which he was, or in the military, which he was, or as responsible monarch, which he was.

I'm not suggesting we can blame all our problems on our parents or spouses, but those closest to us have the power, in their words or actions, to set us up for failure or to release our potential.

I have a deep conviction that lies at the heart of this entire book. Every person needs someone to believe in them, and without that affirmation, they live below their potential. It's difficult to act like a prince when you feel like a failure. It's hard to come into your full potential when you don't feel like you have any.

Princes were born to become kings. Princesses were born to become Queens. But in the Body of Christ, though we were born into the Kingdom of God, our royal inheritance can be for naught if we continue to live beggarly lives of insignificance. We were meant to reign as kings and queens with Christ. Jesus is not only a King, He's the King of Kings, and we are part of that inheritance.

Someone needs to speak prophetically to us so that the full potential of our inheritance can spring into life. Romans 8:17 says that *we are heirs of God and joint (equal) heirs with Jesus Christ*. That's unbelievable. Can you imagine anything more powerful? The Creator of the Universe deigns to share His royal lineage, inheritance, authority, power, dominion, wealth and glory with us. But God has designed the human race, and those of His Kingly Kingdom in particular, to need the build-up of others who see royal blood flowing in his veins. It's not enough to know that we are royalty; we must be raised in a royal environment.

I am convinced that our words can prophetically light the fire of significance in our spouses and families. Children don't need to spend their entire lives feeling insignificant. Wives don't need to spend their lives with unfulfilled potential.

Could my wife have become the globally recognized speaker, author and leader that she is today without me? Quite possibly. She might have done it on her own initiative without anyone's assistance. But for most people, God uses others to stoke the fire of creativity in us. A word of affirmation, a compliment, clarity of direction, reward for work well done, all become incendiary when it relates to a person's potential. Someone gave us an opportunity that opened bigger doors. Someone gave us a contact that proved life-changing. Someone spoke a word of encouragement that shattered years of previous negative statements.

The very term, "Self-made Man" (or woman) I find to be highly suspect. I don't know of anyone who ever lived who can make that boast. We all stand on the shoulders of those who have gone before us. We all were assisted in some way by people who saw potential in us and whose input and affirmation became crucial in our success. If you locate someone you consider to be self-made, I volunteer to look for others in their lives who gave them the boost.

Devi is the most important person in my life. She's my Princess. But I wanted to see her accede to the throne in our home and marriage and become Queen. Actually, I think she's been there for years. I treat her with the dignity and respect that I think is due to royalty. My words accentuate her dignity and my actions promote her royalty. She's godly, glorious and righteous. I'm so blessed to be married to a Queen.

Jesus made it clear, in John 5:31, that others are needed to establish your position in God's Kingdom. *"If I alone bear witness about myself, my testimony is not true."* Then He goes on to state who those other confirming voices are: The Word of God, The works of God, the Father and John the Baptist. Notice that of the 4 voices necessary to confirm someone's status, in this case, Jesus, one is a flesh-and-blood human being, John the Baptist. So it is today; regardless of how much quality, potential, or talent I might have, it always requires another person to bring the liberating voice of confirmation.

I want to be that voice, first to my wife, then to my children and their families, and lastly to everyone I meet. Something powerful happens when you speak life into the smoldering vision of others; it flares and ignites power within them. What greater honor than to let princes know that they were born for greatness, and speak that greatness into them, so they can transition into Kings.

The most oft-repeated words that I speak to people are: You're awesome! And I mean it. Occasionally, someone will rebuke me and say, "Only God is awesome," but I'm quick to remind them that if an awesome God created me, then what does that make me? How can God make me any less than awesome?

Devi and I finished speaking at a Bible College recently and a student came up to us and said, "That was the first time I have ever seen a preacher kiss his wife from the pulpit?"

Maybe the student was just not widely exposed, or maybe he was. How sad. Maybe preachers think that it's only their spoken word that counts. I think our actions are actually more vocal than our sermons. When my son, Aaron, was young, he said to a friend one day, "My parents are frisky." I don't know what that means, but I take it as a compliment.

I know that the kiss from the princess awakened the prince in the frog, in fairy tale lore, and I think it might work for me as well. Devi's love for me awakens the best in me, and I'm sure it's vice-versa. We must do all in our power to bring out royalty in each other.

I pray that in some small way, the fragrance of our marriage has rubbed off on you. Through the medium of books, our lives will live much longer than we will. Should Jesus tarry, I pray that couples, generations from now, will continue to grow through the words in this book.

We are nearing the time when we will board our chariot and ride off toward

137

our heavenly royal palace, The New Jerusalem. Let these, sir, be your final words, "I have loved my wife, my queen, as Jesus loved His church, His Bride, and died for her."

I think I hear the Master respond as your chariot rolls toward the heavenly gates, "*Well done, good and faithful servant. Enter in to the joy of your Lord.*" Wow! I didn't know that our life on earth was just preparation for living as the Bride of Christ forever, just like the Prince and Princess in fairy tale lore, in the New Jerusalem. But the spinners of folk tales were right about one thing: we will live happily ever after, with Jesus our Prince and King of Kings.

P.S. By the way, before you board your chariot, be sure and open the door for your Queen.

12

[SHE Says]
⊕

NO ONE WINS ALONE
By: Devi

I T WAS DURING the heart wrenching, lean and forsaken times that Larry
and I talked about our future and what we wanted to glean from our deep
disappointments and darkest hours. It was important to us to finish well.
Our children were young and we were filled with vision and lots of determination. However, God stopped our progress. He had to process our character
with trials. It was tough, but we clung together and together we stand. We
became stronger in our faith, our calling, our values and our mission. We
embraced our trials and our trials have become our triumphs.

It's not how you begin, but how you finish that counts in life. Wrongs will
be done by you and to you. If you focus on the wrong that was done to you,
you will live in blame and accusation; if you focus on the wrong that you did,
you will be trapped in guilt and shame. So where should your focus be when
thing don't go your way?

> *In Him we have redemption through his blood, the forgiveness
> of our trespasses, according to the riches of his grace, which he
> lavished upon us, in all wisdom and insight making known to us
> the mystery of his will, according to his purpose which he set forth
> in Christ as a plan for the fullness of time, to unite all things in
> him, things in heaven and things on earth.* Ephesians 1:7-10

It was tough, but we clung together and
together we stand.

The Word of God is so powerful and practical. Grasp the concept of *"the
riches of His grace"* and clutch this to your heart. When you, your spouse or
others are wrong, filter this wrongful behavior through *His grace*. Daily do

what Jesus taught us to do, *"…forgive us our debts (trespasses) as we forgive our debtors (those who trespass against us)."* Matthew 6:12

Meditating and praying in this way will change your character. Your focus will no longer be in the moment of shock, shame, sorrow or sadness, but extending the *riches of grace.* Giving favor where it is not deserved will help you to refocus your energy. A grace-focused person is a person who puts the pain of others before their own feelings. Grace-eyes can look beyond the circumstance at hand to see what things can be in the future—not what they are in the present. It is at the point of committing a trespass in our personal lives that Jesus lavishes His grace on us, *"in all wisdom and insight, making known to us the mystery of his will, according to his purpose… "* Ephesians 1:8-9

> We embraced our trials and our trials have become our triumphs.

Grace gives you a future and reveals the mystery of God's will to you for the fulfillment of His purpose in your lives. Giving grace to your spouse gives them hope for their future. But along the path of embracing our trials before they became our triumphs, I had to make some very serious choices. I realized that in many ways, the outcome of our future was in my hands.

During these seasons, and there were more than one, I learned a very valuable principle. This principle became my plumb line in my relationship with Larry. The principle was learned from a Proverb: *"An excellent wife is the crown of her husband but she who shames him is as rottenness in his bones"* (Proverbs 12:4). Larry was always my prince and I was his princess, but I could choose to be a *crown* to him and make him my King or I could chose to *shame* my prince and bring him to absolute uselessness. Larry's future was in my hands.

> A grace-focused person is a person who puts the pain of others before their own feelings.

The word "rotten", used in this Proverb, symbolizes an act of slow decay or deterioration. The imagery that comes to mind is food that is left in my refrigerator too long. When I chose to save it to use for another time, it was still delicious, colorful and full of good nutrients. However, left neglected, the appearance changed. What were once colorful, like bright orange buttery carrots, become distorted greenish-grey, fussy, smelly carrots. What was once full of life and nutrition is now "rotten", no longer good or useful to anyone—it must be discarded.

Understanding this revelation of my responsibility for our future was huge. Is this what I want for Larry? Is it really true that if I neglect him, I have this kind of power over him? That this incredible man that I married could, over time, be reduced to uselessness with no future value to anyone? Could his ministry be discarded? Is this what this scripture means to me?

I believed it and assumed my responsibility. This understanding kept me working on myself, becoming more excellent in all of my ways; seeking God for my strength and wisdom, disciplining my careless tongue, and being certain that my words and actions would not bring embarrassment or shame to him. This raised my standard of behavior to one that I would not have otherwise achieved.

When couples face devastating trials, it is so easy for the wife to point a finger, blame, give advice, accuse, or shame her husband for not protecting them from such pain. But if we do this, it will destroy your spouse. He will lose his initiative, his confidence, his self esteem and wither into nothingness. This does not have to happen. Oh, I don't mean that we will not experience bouts of discouragement or even depression, but when we do, we can look beyond our circumstances and see a future—a man that I will love and unite with. We will spend our future together.

I am not satisfied with just a Prince. I want a King. If an *excellent wife* can be a crown to her husband's head as Proverbs 12:4 says and I want my husband to be crowned KING, then guess what. I have some work to do. I asked myself the question: Do I choose excellence for him or shame for him? My behavior, my words, my attitude, my commitment, my covenant, my morals, my character, my faith will make a difference and determine who Larry becomes.

> I am not satisfied with just a Prince. I want a King.

As I write, the 2012 Summer Olympics are in London. Larry and I are addicted to cheering on our American teams and inspired by the global young people who have disciplined their lives to reach this fierce competition. They are all champions. Piers Morgan, on CNN, interviewed several past gold medal winners. I took notice of two comments by two of the athletes: Michael Duane Johnson (born September 13, 1967) is a retired American sprinter. He won four Olympic gold medals and eight World Championships gold medals.

Johnson currently holds the world and Olympic records in the 400 m and 4 x 400 m relay and is known as the world's fastest runner. He said, "No one wins alone." He continued to say that all winners must have someone who believes in them: a parent, a coach, a teacher, a wife, a husband.

Greg Louganis, considered the greatest diver of all time, won gold medals at the 1984 and 1988 Olympic Games on both the springboard and platform. He is the only male and the second diver in Olympic history to sweep the diving events in consecutive Olympic Games. Greg Louganis, while competing for the gold in Seoul Olympic Games in 1988, hit his head on the diving board. His confidence was shattered. He had to make the decision whether or not to dive again and continue in the Olympic competition. His coach said to him, "You may not believe in yourself, but I believe in you. Dive." Greg competed and went home a champion. In a way, his coach crowned him King of diving before Greg jumped off the board.

No one wins alone.

Be the one to believe in your spouse. I believe in Larry and I have crowned him *King*. I hold him in the highest place in my life. He is above my parents, children and grandchildren. They honor him because I honor him. I celebrate his achievements and support him in his failures. I believe in him when he does not believe in himself. I encourage him to try again and he does the same for me.

Larry treats me like a Queen. I am not a queen; I am the crown of my King. A crown is an ornamental headdress that symbolizes authority. (It's no wonder that I love lots of ornaments.) The crown of a monarch also signifies loyalty to the laws they represent. Larry lives by the laws of God and His grace in our marriage and I reflect my embrace of those laws and his authority by being his crown. The King and his crown are inseparable.

Although physically there may be some hours in the days of a king where the crown is set aside, it is always part of who he is. A KING is never without a crown; he is never without the impact in his life that the crown represents. In the same way, although Larry and I may be a continent apart, he is never without the influence of his crown and I am never without the safeguard of my King.

Some years ago, I was invited to serve on a prestigious Board of Directors. For a while, I was the only woman serving among 19 men. When I attended these meetings, several days long in another state, I was fully aware that my presence was representing Larry. Although Larry was not invited to serve in this position, he fully supported me and was proud of me. While I was an independent thinker and contributor to the decisions and discussions of the business at hand, I knew that my conduct, my conversations, my attire, and my attitude represented not only me, but also my husband. I was his crown and we were inseparable in our influence.

Recently, I was the cover feature of a Brazilian magazine. In the interview, I was asked what my biggest dream is. My biggest dream, in this season of my life, is that couples will know the awesome fulfillment of a life together that is filled with God's love and peace, giving them the fullness of joy. Our legacy is to leave you, two strong leaders, wisdom and truth on how you can thrive in your marriage. What has been possible for us is also possible for you. Larry and I do not want you to say, "No one ever told us." We want to leave a legacy of possibility to you. Now, *we* have told you.

> *...let us also lay aside every weight, and sin which clings so closely, and let us run with endurance the race that is set before us, looking to Jesus, the founder and perfecter of our faith....* Hebrews 12:1-2

If you think that no one else believes in you, you are wrong. *We believe in you.* How your marriage began is not the issue now. It is how you finish. Embrace the truths that are in this book, use our lives as your example and finish what you have started—finish well. And ladies, when the Chariots of Fire arrive at your door, may you say, "I reverenced my husband and gave him honor in the same way the church gives glory to Christ." Don yourselves with royal robes of marriage success and thrive—together. Your kingdom of generations to come will be blessed.

IF YOU'RE A FAN OF THIS BOOK, PLEASE TELL OTHERS...

+ Write about *When Leaders Live Together* on your blog, Twitter, MySpace, and Facebook page.
+ Suggest *When Leaders Live Together* to friends.
+ When you're in a bookstore, ask them if they carry the book. The book is available through all major distributors, so any bookstore that does not have *When Leaders Live Together* in stock, can easily order it.
+ Write a positive review of *When Leaders Live Together* on www.amazon.com.
+ Send my publisher, HigherLife Publishing, suggestions on Web sites, conferences, and events you know of where this book could be offered at media@ahigherlife.com.
+ Purchase additional copies to give away as gifts.

CONNECT WITH ME...

To schedule Larry Titus in your church, please contact:

Kingdom Global Ministries
2250 Pool Rd. Ste. 200
Grapevine, TX 76051
phone: 817-251-0333

email: info@kingdomglobal.com
web: www.Kingdomglobal.com

Or contact my publisher directly:

HigherLife Publishing
400 Fontana Circle, Building 1—Suite 105
Oviedo, Florida 32765
Phone: (407) 563-4806
Email: media@ahigherlife.com